The First Nations Longhouse

Verna J. Kirkness and Jo-ann Archibald

The First Nations Longhouse

Our Home Away from Home

Printed in Canada on acid-free paper

ISBN 0-88865-788-9

**National Library of Canada Cataloguing in
Publication Data**

Kirkness, Verna J., 1935-
    The First Nations Longhouse

    ISBN 0-88865-788-9

    1. First Nations Longhouse (Vancouver, BC) –
History. 2. Indian architecture – British Columbia.
I. Archibald, Jo-ann, 1950- II. University of British
Columbia. First Nations House of Learning.
III. Title.

E78.B9K527 2001   728'.089'970711   C2001-910378-6

The First Nations House of Learning gratefully
acknowledges financial support from the Vice
President Academic and Provost's Office, the
University of British Columbia, and from David
Bellman, X̱wi7x̱wa. Proceeds from the sale of this
book go to First Nations student bursaries, awards,
and scholarships.

Printed and bound in Canada by Friesens
Set in Trinité and Meta
Designer: George Vaitkunas
Editor: Camilla Jenkins
Proofreader: Darlene Money
p. ii, Ceremonial door, Photo: Steven Evans;
p. vi, Outside the longhouse, Photo: Jack G.M. Wong;
pp. 2-3, Longhouse, Photo: George Vaitkunas

First Nations House of Learning
University of British Columbia
1985 West Mall
Vancouver, BC V6T 1Z2
(604) 822-8940
www.longhouse.ubc.ca

Tsimilano's Teaching

My dear ones,

Form a circle and join hands in prayer. In joining hands, hold your left palm upward to reach back to grasp the teachings of the Ancestors. Hold your right palm downward to pass these teachings on to the younger generation. In this way, the teachings of the Ancestors continue and the circle of human understanding and caring grows stronger.

Contents

Foreword

N<small>I-JING-JADA</small>, "the Longhouse Lady," is the name that Haida Elder Minnie Croft bestowed on Verna Kirkness, as it was through her vision and tireless effort that the longhouse was built. Verna arrived at the University of British Columbia in 1981 and demonstrated leadership in the Native Indian Teacher Education Program (N<small>ITEP</small>) and the *Tsʷkel* graduate program. Through the First Nations House of Learning, she worked to extend support services and cultural inclusion to Native students in all UBC programs. Jo-ann Archibald, who followed Verna as the director of the First Nations House of Learning, has served in this capacity for the past eight years. She is a wonderful role model for First Nations students and her contribution toward making the longhouse a "home away from home" is notable.

Sharing characterizes the First Nations Longhouse. All who enter are reminded of the amazing richness of North American Aboriginal cultures. Whether it is a story told in the housepost carvings, an Elder's account of growing up on the coast, or participating in a feast to mark an important event, every person who comes to the longhouse is enriched by the traditions that are readily shared by the longhouse family of Elders, students, and staff.

We are proud to be part of the "Longhouse family." We first met in 1954 at UBC, one an undergraduate Law student, the other a freshman in Agriculture. One became the university's first Native graduate in Law, the other the University's Vice-President Academic and Provost. Both of us played a role in advancing First Nations programs and we were happy to be involved in the building of the longhouse.

Sty-Wet-Tan (the great hall) in Hun'q'umin'um means "spirit of the west wind," which welcomes people from the four directions. This is what the longhouse does.

The story told here by Verna and Jo-ann honours the traditions of their people.

A<small>LFRED</small> S<small>COW</small> (P<small>UNGWIDI</small>)   D<small>ANIEL</small> R. B<small>IRCH</small> (M<small>ITÊHE</small>)
Elder and Judge (retired)   Vice-President Academic and Provost Emeritus

Preface

EVER SINCE I RETIRED from the University of British Columbia in 1993, I have wanted to write a book about the building of the First Nations Longhouse. I had a number of reasons. First, I wanted it to be known that First Nations Elders, students, faculty, and staff had been instrumental in defining the purpose and concept of the longhouse and had steered the process to its completion. Second, I thought it was important to acknowledge the donors, whose philanthropic effort made the longhouse possible. Third, it was significant, also, to acknowledge the university for responding to our request to build a longhouse on campus for First Nations students. The University of British Columbia set a precedent not only in having a culturally sensitive building for its First Nations students but also in entrusting First Nations people to direct and guide the project. This truly gave us a sense of ownership of the longhouse. As proprietors, those who make the longhouse their home continue to care for it in a very special way.

Over the years, there have been many requests from people at colleges, universities, and First Nations communities interested in building a facility that reflects First Nations traditional architecture. Questions about fundraising and the planning process were asked time and again. It seemed important to record this information for the benefit of others wanting to build similar learning structures.

Unfortunately, or perhaps fortunately, I procrastinated in working on the book. It was not until 1998 that I prepared a proposal to set the project in motion. I was, however, in a quandary about how to rationalize writing about the longhouse that had been completed five years before. Then it occurred to me that another part of this story should be told. It was now possible to describe the experience of life at the longhouse. With that thought, I approached Jo-ann Archibald, who had succeeded me as the director of the First Nations House of Learning, to write this part. As a result, I wrote the first section of the book, about creating the dream, and she gave an account of living the dream daily in the longhouse. We chose these themes because we felt fortunate in having a significant dream and being able to achieve it.

This book, then, is our attempt to provide an account of the people, the events, and the process involved in the creation of the longhouse and subsequently, to share what life is like within the longhouse. It is also a record of the many ceremonies held to mark important intervals, beginning with the raising of the signpost in May 1990.

As I worked on this book, I was often very frustrated with trying to recall the details of the process and of various events. Though I could refer to several files, I wished that I had kept a journal. Nevertheless, with the help of many people, we were able to get the book completed.

We would like to acknowledge other contributors to this book, for if it were not for their newsletter articles, we would be bereft of important information. Thank you to our colleagues Madeleine MacIvor, Verena (Cootes) Wilhelmson, Sharilyn Calliou, and student Bruce Marjoribanks, all of whom contributed invaluable articles to the commemorative issue of the 1993 *First Nations House of Learning Newsletter.* Thank you Shirley Sterling, for the detailed description you prepared of the artists and their carved houseposts and roof-end beams for the Sty-Wet-Tan rentals booklet. Thank you Marjorie Simmins, for your article in the 1992 *UBC Alumni Chronicle* for your apt description of the longhouse roof as "the wings of a bird in flight."

We are grateful for the willing assistance of Larry McFarland, the principal architect, for diligently reviewing sections of the manuscript, the content of which only he was qualified to assess. Thank you Larry, for all your help and for providing many of the photographs we have included in the book. Thank you Bill McLennan, for your time and effort in helping to complete the story of the carvers and the carving project. As well, the photographs you provided for the book are appreciated.

Thank you Pamela Miles, for your help in writing about the World of Opportunity Campaign and the donors. I enjoyed working with you as we tried to secure dollars for the longhouse.

Tom Berger and Carolyn Kenny, you did a great job as reviewers and critics of my many drafts. Without your constructive comments and encouragement, I doubt that this book would have been written. Thanks a million.

As you look at this book, the first thing you will notice is that it contains pages and pages of beautiful photographs. There is great truth to the adage that a picture is worth a thousand words. We are grateful that so many people took photographs throughout the project. We have not only used photographs by Larry McFarland and Bill McLennan, but also want to thank the following people for contributing photographs for the book: Pam Brown; John Chong and Martin Dee at UBC ITServices, Telestudios; Pat Higinbotham – Studio 54; Greg Morton, Janis Franklin, and Michael Robertson at The Media Group, Woodward Instructional Resources Centre, UBC; Bill Keay of the *Vancouver Sun;* Beverley Berger; Steven Evans; Alan Katowitz; Malak; David Neel; Angie Oleman; George Vaitkunas; Tania Wahbe; Bentley Wong; and Jack G.M. Wong.

Thanks to those who helped me to remember. This includes the above-mentioned as well as Chief Simon Baker, Alfred and Joan Scow, Ethel Gardner, Felicity Jules, Sheila TeHennepe, and Monty Palmatier.

Finally, thanks Jo-ann, for co-authoring this book with me. It was definitely meant to be, as collectively we have been a part of the dream and the life of the longhouse for well over a decade. I know that we share pride in having worked on this book, which is the property of the First Nations House of Learning.

Jo-ann and I are pleased to announce that all proceeds from the sale of *The First Nations Longhouse: Our Home Away from Home* will be used to support bursaries, awards, and scholarships to First Nations students at the University of British Columbia.

Verna J. Kirkness

Chronology

26 January 1989	First official meeting of students, staff, and Elders to discuss the concept of a longhouse at UBC
1 March 1989	A second meeting to brainstorm about what should be contained in the longhouse
17 March 1989	Jack Bell donates $1,000,000 to UBC for First Nations
12 May 1989	First Nations House of Learning Advisory Committee members unanimously agree to allocate Jack Bell's donation to the construction of the longhouse; the President's Office approves
5 October 1989	First meeting of the Longhouse Building Committee
17 October 1989	Three architectural firms interviewed
31 October 1989	Larry McFarland Architects Ltd. selected
November-December 1989	Building Committee meets architect to discuss process, scheduling, site, and funding
11 January 1990	First of series of workshops with students, Elders, staff, and Building Committee, with the topic "Identity"
25 January 1990	Second workshop, "Functions"
8 February 1990	Third workshop, "Site"
22 February 1990	Fourth workshop, "Image"
1 March 1990	Workshop results assessed
22 March 1990	Tour and evaluation of possible sites; site selected
5 April 1990	Architects present pre-design brief to Building Committee
17 April 1990	Building Committee and architect meet Musqueam Band Council at Musqueam Reserve
26 April 1990	Workshop to discuss functional program
23 May 1990	Building Committee reviews functional program draft
29 May 1990	Site dedication ceremony
13 June 1990	Architect presents schematic design brief
27 July 1990	Ground blessing ceremony
31 May 1991	Sod turning ceremony
17 July 1992	Houseposts unveiling and roof-beam raising ceremony
13 March 1993	Longhouse cleansing ceremony
15 March 1993	Move into the longhouse
25 May 1993	Grand opening of longhouse

The First Nations Longhouse

Creating the Dream

Verna J. Kirkness

The Grand Opening of the First Nations Longhouse

Grandmothers, grandfathers, sisters, brothers, and grandchildren from the four directions, welcome to the First Nations Longhouse at the University of British Columbia. We are honoured that you have journeyed here from far and near to witness this special occasion and to join with us in our celebration. We thank the Great Spirit for bringing you safely to us and for giving us this beautiful day that we may unite in love and harmony. The longhouse is a symbol of love, harmony, and a strong belief in a spiritual power that makes all things possible. From the fall of 1988, our students, our Elders, our faculty and staff, representing many different First Nations, worked together through long hours of meetings and workshops to provide direction and guidance to the building of this longhouse.

We wanted the longhouse to be our home away from home, where children and Elders had a prominent place in the daily lives of the students.

We wanted the longhouse to be a place where our heritage would be respected and where our cultures could thrive.

We wanted the longhouse to be a place where we could share our knowledge and cultures with one another.

We wanted the longhouse to be a place where we could share our knowledge and cultures with the university community and with the larger society.

Today, we gather to celebrate a dream come true, a vision to benefit those with us now and those children who are yet unborn. On behalf of the students, Elders, faculty, and staff, I lift my hands in praise and thanksgiving to every person who was involved in any way in the creation of this magnificent longhouse that stands here today.

Thank you to each and every one of you who have come to witness and celebrate with us.

It was 25 May 1993, the grand opening of the First Nations Longhouse on the University of British Columbia campus. An audience of hundreds had come to join in the celebration. I can still remember the feeling I had as the realization hit me. Our dream was fulfilled. We had our longhouse and it was even

Verna J. Kirkness delivers her opening address at the grand opening of the longhouse.
Photo: UBC ITServices, Telestudios

Facing previous page:
Over 1,000 guests attended the 25 May 1993 opening.
Photo: David Neel

Below: A drummer at the grand opening.
Photo: UBC ITServices, Telestudios

more magnificent than I had expected. It seemed that all the world was there rejoicing with us. It was a wonderful time for our people! As I gave my welcome address, it was a moment of pride, joy, and excitement.

This spectacular, 2,043 square metre Coast Salish-style longhouse, the first of its kind on a North American university campus, would serve as a "home away from home" for Aboriginal students attending UBC. To have a place of our own, in an institute of higher learning, was a major accomplishment in the journey of our people. Constructed of West Coast red cedar logs, the longhouse is a symbol of the traditional dwellings of the Coast Salish people, providing our students with an appropriate learning environment.

The opening celebration began with a procession known as a grand entry, a practice common to many First Nations in North America to mark the start of an important event. In the procession were many of the people who had played a role in realizing this dream. Our Elders, our First Nations graduates, our faculty and staff, the major donors, university and government dignitaries, the architects, and the artists, along with special guests from other countries, walked proudly to the beat of the drum onto the ceremonial plaza.

The crowd of people gathered to witness this event seemed to be drawn in to the sight and sound of the

procession. Many of us wore traditional regalia, showing the pride we felt on this day as First Nations people and in the longhouse that stood as a reminder of our heritage. For me, it was the first time I had worn the full regalia of a Cree woman. The white buckskin dress, the moccasins, the beaded belt, and the feather in my hair all contributed to a sense of wholeness for me and a tremendous sense of achievement.

Once the people in the procession were seated, Jo-ann Archibald, our spokesperson for the occasion, introduced Vince Stogan, Elder of the Musqueam Nation, who brought greetings from his people, on whose traditional territory the university is situated. He offered a prayer of thanksgiving to the Creator for the gift of the longhouse. UBC President David Strangway and I, as director of the First Nations House

Clockwise, from upper left:

Jo-ann Archibald, spokesperson for the longhouse grand opening.
Photo: UBC ITServices, Telestudios

Justin Campbell and Linda Haig-Brown hold a cedar rope, which will be cut to signify the official opening of the First Nations Longhouse.
Photo: David Neel

Verna J. Kirkness and President David Strangway after cutting the rope to signify the official opening of the First Nations Longhouse.
Photo: UBC ITServices, Telestudios

Premier Mike Harcourt, Elder Vince Stogan giving welcoming words, President David Strangway.
Photo: David Neel

Top: Kwakwaka'wakw dance group performs at the ceremony.
Photo: UBC ITServices, Telestudios

Bottom: Premier Mike Harcourt, President David Strangway, Chief Simon Baker, Maori Elder Rangimarie Rose Pere from New Zealand, and UBC Chancellor Leslie Peterson.
Photo: David Neel

of Learning, cut the cedar rope to the applause of the audience as we declared the First Nations Longhouse at UBC "open."

After my welcome address, Elder Alfred Scow of the Kwakwaka'wakw Nation, President Strangway, Premier Mike Harcourt, Maori spiritual leader Rangimarie Rose Pere, and Robin Woodhead, of Tsimshian ancestry and the first Aboriginal graduate of the Faculty of Medicine, brought greetings.

Interspersed throughout the program were spectacular dance performances by various First Nations. The children of Seabird Island School, Agassiz, BC, sang a song in their Halq'emeylem language affirming the reality of the longhouse as a place wherein their languages would have a respected place.

Three plaques were unveiled. One was an acknowledgement by the university that the longhouse was located on the traditional territory of the Musqueam people. The second announced the grand opening of the First Nations Longhouse, and the third provided a list of the donors who had made financial contributions to the building fund.

Elder Minnie Croft and Robin
Woodhead at the grand opening.
Robin was the first Aboriginal
graduate of the Faculty of
Medicine at UBC.
Photo: UBC ITServices, Telestudios

Joe Alec leads the Seabird Island
School children's group.
Photo: UBC ITServices, Telestudios

President David Strangway and Elder Vince Stogan unveil a plaque acknowledging that the university is on Musqueam traditional territory.
Photo: UBC ITServices, Telestudios

Chancellor W. Robert Wyman and Chief Simon Baker unveil a plaque commemorating the longhouse opening.
Photo: David Neel

Robert Davidson leads the
Rainbow Creek Dancers, of the
Haida Nation.

Photos: UBC ITServices, Telestudios

Top: William Bellman receives the name X̱wi7x̱wa from Chief Simon Baker, of the Squamish Nation. Chief Baker sings a traditional Squamish song.
Photo: David Neel

Bottom: Paddle given to William Bellman.
Photo: George Vaitkunas

Non-Aboriginal society has a custom of naming buildings after major donors. Among many Aboriginal societies a similar practice is observed. Naming ceremonies are held to pass on ancestral names, usually to younger family members. On other occasions, names are given to those who have performed an extraordinary function in respect of the people, or names may be given to acknowledge significant events or achievements.

We had several occasions to give names to particular people who were instrumental in opening doors for us to have the longhouse. On each of these occasions, much consideration and consultation went on among the Elders who would bestow the name. Our first naming ceremony had been held in May 1991 during the sod turning ceremony, to honour Jack Bell, who was our first major donor. The other two major donors, William Bellman and James Wallace, received their names during the grand opening of the longhouse.

Chief Simon Baker and his wife, Emily, were called to the podium. Chief Baker bestowed the Squamish name X̱wi7x̱wa, pronounced "whei wha," on William Bellman, who had donated $1 million to the project. Chief Baker explained:

X̱wi7x̱wa means "echo" in our language. When our people travelled in the early days, the echo served as a compass. When a person hollered, the "echo" let you know how far you were from the beach. There is a story, which is very long, that has been handed down over the years about X̱wi7x̱wa. When you hear the story, you draw your own conclusions about its teaching. If you ever have lots of time, come over, and I'll tell you the whole story.

I believe the name X̱wi7x̱wa is the right name for you because of your early work in radio and television, which like the echo was a way to communicate. The library will carry your name and be known as X̱wi7x̱wa Library in your honour. I feel that the library is very important to the students who are studying here. It will be a place where they can read about what our people did in the past.

I give you this paddle to help you in the future. Don't leave home without it! My wife gives you this drum to remember this occasion.

Sm'oogit Niiyeesgiminuu Alvin Weget, Sm'oogit Geel Walter Harris and his wife, Sadie, Sm'oogit Wii Alast Jim Angus of the Gitx̱san Nation, with witness Sm'oogit Alfred Joseph of the Wet'suwet'en Nation, made their way to the podium for the naming of James Wallace, who had donated $500,000 to enable the completion of the longhouse. The Gitx̱san name conferred on him was Wii Ax. The administrative area of the longhouse would be named Wii Ax because of his life-long interest in administration.

A plaque in X̱wi7x̱wa Library acknowledges the kindness of William and June Bellman.

Photo: Bentley Wong

A Gitxsan and Wet'suwet'en delegation bestows the name Wii Ax on James Wallace.

Sadie Harris, speaking on behalf of the Gitxsan Nation, made the presentation:

Our Gitxsan names originate from strange happenings, from supernatural happenings or even from spiritual happenings or sightings. So it is with the name you are being given today.

A long time ago, a large group of people who were travelling on a road decided to make camp for the evening as it was getting quite dark. The men started to collect what wood they could. They did not really notice what kind of stumps, branches, or debris they threw on the fire. Soon it was huge and roaring! It provided whatever light was needed along with the heat needed to cook their evening meal. The fire kept to its strength long into the night. In the morning they noticed a plant standing firm right in the middle of what was left of their fire from the night before! It mystified them. Not only was it far away from its natural habitat, [but] it [had] withstood a roaring fire. What special plant was it? What powers did it have? From that time on, Wii Ax was claimed as the family crest of Guu Wo'otxw in the House of Gutk'uunuxws.

On behalf of the Gitxsan Nation of the Skeena River, Sm'oogit Niiyeesgiminuu, Mr Alvin Weget, who is a member of the House, has graciously offered to bestow upon Mr James Wallace the name Wii Ax. In our tradition, Mr Wallace will be a true brother to him. He has the right to sit at Mr Weget's feast table should he be in Hazelton or Kispiox for special occasions.

The blanket is his. He has the right to use it whenever there is a call to do so, but it is Mr Weget's wish that it remains in its place of honour at the First Nations House of Learning forever, to be a reminder to the Elders, students, faculty, staff, and guests who pass through its doors, of the substantial gift given by Mr and Mrs James Wallace.

We are indeed grateful, and we, in turn, give you this highest honour we could possibly give you because we are investing in our children. When they enter this building they will feel right at home and for this we thank you.

Elder Minnie Croft of the House of Skedans, Haida Gwaii, and her niece Terri-Lynn Williams stood to confer the Haida name Kil Sli on Dr David Strangway. Placing a beautiful Haida blanket on Dr Strangway, Minnie began:

I have the pleasant and enjoyable duty of presenting our eagle ceremonial blanket and a new Haida name to the President of the University of British Columbia, Dr David Strangway. My niece, Terri-Lynn Williams, a UBC graduate in computer science and now in the law program, will help me with this presentation.

I'd like to tell you a little story in connection with the name we are bestowing on Dr Strangway. Once when I was interpreting in the Supreme Court of British Columbia, the Haida petitioner called the judge "Kil Sli" and the judge asked me to explain the name. In the Haida language, "Kil Sli" is a name bestowed on a

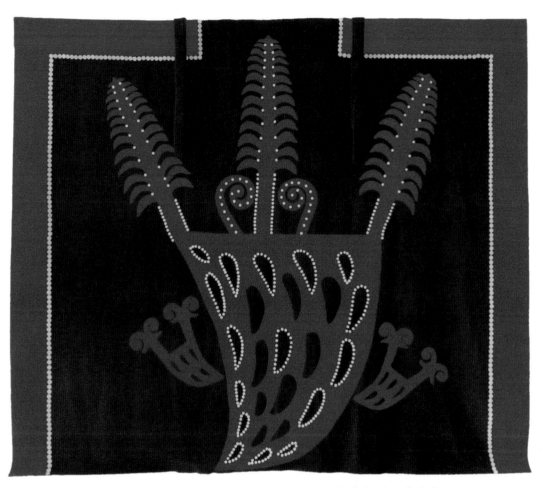

Sadie Harris made the button blanket given to James Wallace at the grand opening.
Photo: Bentley Wong

15

person who we feel deserves a high honour. The judge in his English way wondered if it could be construed as a bribe. No, Dr Strangway, we Haida do not bribe when we give you our fine name. You are a great man! Without your commitment to our Native people, we would not be standing by this very beautiful longhouse today.

Elders Dr and Mrs Ahab Spence and I, with witnesses Kathy Louis and Elder Margaret White, conferred the name Mitêhe on Dr Daniel R. Birch, Vice President Academic and Provost of the University of British Columbia. I acknowledged Dr Birch, saying,

In recognition of the compassion, understanding, and commitment of Daniel R. Birch to the advancement of Aboriginal education, we bestow on him the name Mitêhe, which in the language of the Cree people means "heart" with the spiritual connotation of "life."

With the support he gave us as Dean of Education and later as Vice President Academic and Provost, progress has been made toward making the University of British Columbia a more relevant and friendly place for Aboriginal students.

The eagle is a symbol of greatness in many Aboriginal societies. The eagle featured in this mandala we are presenting to you is a fitting token of our appreciation to Dr Birch.

The presentation is made on behalf of the students, faculty, and staff at the grand opening of the First Nations Longhouse, on May 25th, 1993.

The naming ceremony was a very moving experience. Watching the faces of the recipients told the story of how proud they were to receive their Aboriginal names. William Bellman and James Wallace were aware that they would be given names. For Dr Strangway and Dr Birch, it was a total surprise. Dr Strangway's shy smile as he was robed in the button blanket and given the name Kil Sli showed his pleasure at being recognized in this traditional manner. It was obvious that Minnie had a very special feeling for this extraordinary man who had made the longhouse project a priority. Dr Birch was so moved at receiving his name that his only comment was, "I don't know of anything that has touched my heart more."

The whole day was one of great emotion and pure excitement for me. I can still picture Oscar, Beverly, Philip, and Ellen, four of our students, approaching the podium and inviting me to join them. While Oscar spoke, Beverly and Ellen draped a beautiful button blanket on me: "On behalf of the students, past, present, and future, we'd like to thank you, Verna. The crest that you see on the button blanket symbolizes the wealth of the Native people. In the copper, we have included the First Nations House of Learning logo. Certainly, Verna, we feel that your contribution to First Nations, especially here in BC, will not be forgotten."

Oscar Swanson, president of the First Nations Student Association, presents Verna J. Kirkness with a button blanket.
Photo: Beverley Berger

I was filled with mixed emotions at this gesture of respect and kindness from the students. I had made the decision to leave UBC after this dream was realized. I had enjoyed my work, and the completion of the longhouse signalled both an end and a beginning. It was time for someone else to take the helm. As a Prairie Cree coming to this university and this province in 1980, I can truly say that I felt accepted and appreciated by the students, which meant a lot to me. I was at home here, with the Aboriginal people of British Columbia.

In continuing with the protocol of the Coast Salish people, and following the oral tradition, all present were considered witnesses to the grand opening of the longhouse and had the responsibility to tell others about what had taken place that day. Four of the witnesses were asked to speak. Patricia Beyer was asked because it was important for her to take the message of the longhouse back to Fisher River, Patricia's and my home reserve in Manitoba. Tom Berger was chosen because he

has always been a strong supporter of Aboriginal rights
and had been our mentor throughout the years that
we worked to create an Aboriginal presence on campus.
His sentiment was poignantly expressed as he spoke:

*This is a place that First Nations students and First Nations
people can call their own today. But it is also another place – the
dwelling place of generations. For what has been achieved today
was made possible by the determination of earlier generations of
First Nations people to survive – not only to survive but to find
for themselves, their children, and their grandchildren, a distinct
and contemporary place in the life of our country.*

*Land claims, self-determination, and all other opportunities
that await First Nations peoples exist because earlier generations
never forgot who they were. They understood that, in Pascal's
phrase, it is essential "to become who you are."*

*The planning, design, and construction of the First Nations
Longhouse is based on the contribution of earlier generations.
It is they who preserved and maintained First Nations cultures,
languages, and claims, enabling them to achieve recognition in
our time. So, as you admire this wondrous new structure, remember that it is, and will remain, the dwelling place of generations.*

Margaret Valadian, a colleague from Australia, was
invited to be a witness because we wanted the message
of the longhouse to reach the Aboriginal people of her

country. The fourth witness to speak was Alfie Waugh, a Chipewyan from the Northwest Territories. Alfie was an architectural student at the university and was employed part time to work on the longhouse. That unique combination of experiences gave him something to share with others along with the story of this special occasion.

The celebration continued with a song composed and sung by Judy (Golar) Nuualiita of the Carrier Nation, a graduating student in the Native Indian Teacher Education Program (NITEP). Her lyrics blended in with a chant, expressing her feelings about the longhouse and the future generations who would find this a home away from home. Her song issued an invitation to come to this place, where everyone would feel welcome. Come, she says, for the quiet, to learn, to teach, to dance, to laugh, to share, and to pray. Deina Jules, a Shuswap student in Ts''kel Graduate Studies, closed the formal part of the ceremony by singing a Shuswap honour song.

The guests then entered Sty-Wet-Tan, the great hall of the longhouse, through the ceremonial eastern door. As they entered, students, staff, and volunteers handed each person a small copper-shaped medallion with the House of Learning logo on it. The medallion was tied to a leather thong so that it could be worn as a necklace.

Top: Witnesses Margaret Valadian, from Australia, Patricia Beyer, Tom Berger, and Alfie Waugh.

Bottom: Deina Jules, of the Shuswap Nation, sings an honour song at the close of the opening ceremony. Jo-ann Archibald and Judy (Golar) Nuualiita stand with her. Judy sang a song called "Our Place of Vision," which she wrote in honour of the First Nations House of Learning and the longhouse.
Photos: David Neel

Our Place of Vision

Composed and sung by Judy (Golar) Nuualiita, 1993

Hey Yah, Hey Yah
Our ancestors would be proud to witness this special day,
The First Nations House of Learning is for learning in the traditional way,
Hey Yah, Hey Yah
With young children, young men and women,
Mothers, fathers and our Elders too...
Hey Yah, Hey Yah
We learn from each other, as we always do
Hey Yah, Hey Yah, Hey Yah, Hey Yah, Hey Yah, Hey Yah *(Repeat twice)*

We stand proud for this Longhouse, where we come together as one
All First Nations are gathered, we are second to none
Hey Yah, Hey Yah
As the eagle soars, so shall this Longhouse stand
For future generations all across this land
Hey Yah, Hey Yah ...
To strengthen our nation, learning will meet the demand
Hey Yah, Hey Yah, Hey Yah, Hey Yah, Hey Yah, Hey Yah *(Repeat twice)*

We thank you and bless you for being here to share with us our dream,
Our new place of vision is real now it seems,
Hey Yah, Hey Yah ...
This is our meeting place here at UBC
We will always welcome everyone we see,
Hey Yah, Hey Yah, Hey Yah, Hey Yah, Hey Yah, Hey Yah *(Repeat twice)*

Come for the quiet, Hey Yah, Hey Yah ...
Come to learn, Hey Yah, Hey Yah ...
Come to teach, Hey Yah, Hey Yah ...
Come for dancing, Hey Yah, Hey Yah ...
Come for laughter, Hey Yah, Hey Yah ...
Come to share, Hey Yah, Hey Yah ...
Come to pray, Hey Yah, Hey Yah, Hey Yah
Hey Yah, Hey Yah, Hey Yah

The inscription on the back read, "Grand Opening of the First Nations Longhouse, UBC, May 25th, 1993."

Everyone was invited to the traditional feast organized by Gitxsan caterer Dolly Watts. The feast table, beautifully laid out in the foyer, featured such delicacies as barbecued salmon, clam fritters, deer, wild rice salad, bannock, and a very large celebration cake. Cases of apples and oranges donated to us from various stores were given away as well.

After the feast, the First Nations students and staff gave presents to the guests. Among the gifts were blankets, limited edition prints, and T-shirts with the First Nations House of Learning logo on them. Many of the guests, in turn, brought gifts for the longhouse. These gifts can be seen, prominently displayed, throughout the building.

It was a very long day, which is typical of celebrations of this kind. The evening ended around midnight after we enjoyed various performances in a celebration of cultures.

It is seven years since the grand opening. Every May 25th, I remember the day and silently celebrate each anniversary knowing that the longhouse is serving the purpose for which it was designed. It truly is a home away from home for Aboriginal students at UBC. Whenever I return for a visit, I am delighted to see

Grand Opening
of the
First Nations Longhouse

PROGRAM

5:30 p.m. Ceremonial Opening

Ceremonial Entry into the First
Nations Longhouse

6:00 p.m. Host – Verna J. Kirkness
Spokesperson – Jo-ann Archibald

Traditional Welcome Dance

Greetings

Elder Alfred J. Scow
First Nations House of Learning

David W. Strangway
*President of the University of
British Columbia*

Mike Harcourt
*Premier, Province of British
Columbia*

Rangimarie Rose Pere
Maori Spiritual Leader

Robin Woodhead
*1993 Graduate Student, Faculty of
Medicine*

Unveiling of Plaques

Naming Ceremony

Witnessing

7:00 p.m. Feast

8:00 p.m. Giveaway
Gifts to the Longhouse

9:00 p.m. Celebration of Cultures

*The Chancellor and the President
of
The University of British Columbia*

and

*The Elders, Students, Faculty and Staff
of The First Nations House of Learning*

cordially invite you to the

Grand Opening
of
The First Nations Longhouse

*Tuesday, May 25, 1993
at 5:30 p.m.*

*1985 West Mall
The University of British Columbia*

*RSVP: May 10, 1993
Reply card enclosed*

Sty-Wet-Tan, the great hall, buzzing with activity. My uncle, Leonard Kirkness, who was present at the opening, asks me how the longhouse is doing when I visit him on the Fisher River reserve. It was wonderful to have him here on that day along with other members of my family and special friends, who came from other provinces to attend. When something significant happens in our lives, the presence of family and friends is vitally important.

Following two pages: Our home away from home.

Photo: George Vaitkunas

The Ceremonies

Six ceremonies marked important stages in the process of building the longhouse. These ceremonies gave us an opportunity to observe the protocol of the Coast Salish and other Aboriginal cultures. Through the teachings of the Elders, we were guided in the traditions of our people and extended these teachings and practices to our university community.

Ceremonies, among our people, are a way of acknowledging important events, a way to record history through oral communication, a way to pass on the culture to succeeding generations, and a time to strengthen the bonds within the community.

The Elders reminded us that we must begin each gathering by forming a circle and joining hands in prayer. The joining of hands is a symbol of strength and unity. The Elders reminded us of the importance of the oral tradition and made witnessing a function of our ceremonies. They explained that while everyone present had the responsibility to pass on to others what they had witnessed, certain people should be officially designated as witnesses and given a token payment. Quarters are usually given today. A witness will be called upon to speak, and as he or she does so the hosts of the gathering may place more quarters in the palm of the speaker's hand to indicate their thanks and respect for what is being said.

Providing food for the occasion is an essential part of each ceremony. We were taught that it is the responsibility of the younger people to serve the Elders first, then those who have come the greatest distance are next, with the hosts always being the last to eat.

As I think of these ceremonies and the project as a whole, I marvel at the way it all seemed to flow and come together. Along the way, in our planning meetings and workshops, many difficult decisions had to be made. Though the Elders, the students, and the staff were of many different cultural backgrounds, this did not influence our judgement. First and foremost, we were preparing a home away from home for all Aboriginal students. Although our decisions favoured the Coast Salish tradition much of the time, we understood why that had to be the case. Elder Vince Stogan reminded us many times that the longhouse, though built in the Musqueam style and located on their traditional territory, was for everyone.

Ceremonies were held to dedicate the site, to bless the ground, to turn the sod to mark the beginning of construction, to raise the houseposts and roof beams, to cleanse the longhouse before occupancy, and to celebrate the official opening of the longhouse. The first milestone in the building of the longhouse was the site dedication ceremony.

Site Dedication, 29 May 1990

Chief Simon Baker opened the ceremony with a song that was given to him by his grandfather, Chief Joe Capilano. Chief Capilano had sung it when a delegation of chiefs went to England in 1906 to appeal to King Edward VII for recognition of their rights in Canada. He told the story of his grandfather's adventure. Chief Baker welcomed the people to the gathering, then blessed and dedicated the site where the longhouse would stand.

A sign designating the site as "the future home of the First Nations Longhouse" was unveiled by UBC President Strangway and Elder Minnie Croft. The importance and significance of the site were acknowledged, after which Tom Berger, co-chair of the First Nations House of Learning Advisory Committee, and President Strangway spoke as witnesses to the event. As the hosts, the First Nations students and staff gave quarters to the witnesses as a gesture of thanks for their kind words. The ceremony ended with refreshments served at the Graduate Student Centre.

We had much to do in the months leading up to the site dedication ceremony. Larry McFarland and his associates conducted a series of "site workshops" with us, in which we considered whom we would like to have as neighbours and whom we would not, our proximity to the hub of the campus, the kind of terrain we wanted, and other aspects related to location. Some questions required debate until a consensus was reached.

In order to determine an appropriate location, the university designated five possible sites for the longhouse. One was near the Museum of Anthropology. It was a beautiful site near English Bay where many eagles and other birds could be found. It would have been ideal in many respects, but it was agreed that this particular site should never have a building on it. The feeling of sacredness about it made the idea of a building seem like an intrusion. We made our view known to the university and asked that the site be preserved in its pristine state. So far that request has been honoured.

The unanimous choice of location for the longhouse was part of the campus arboretum then used for a parking lot. It was, ideally, located near the heart of the campus. The arboretum is a teaching forest of species from around the world that was planted over eighty years ago when the university was established. As the architectural firm's project description noted, the deciduous trees to the south would provide shelter for the interior of the longhouse from the sun in summer and with the shedding of their leaves allow light into the building during the winter months.

Students, staff, and Elders tour the university grounds with David Wilkinson of Larry McFarland Architects to select the longhouse site.

Photo: Larry McFarland Architects

The coniferous trees to the north would impart a tranquil, reflective mood and a gentle quality of light. A longhouse placed at the proper axis would ensure minimal interference with the variety of trees. Only five trees had to be removed. Three were transplanted and the others were used in the landscaping.

Just two months later, we held our second ceremony.

Ground Blessing, 27 July 1990

The ground blessing was different from most of the other ceremonies we held as it was a Musqueam sacred ceremony conducted entirely according to tradition. Elder Vince Stogan and his wife, Edna, assisted by Steven Point and Jo-ann Archibald of the Sto:lo Nation, performed the ceremony. A fire was lit and prayers were offered to the Creator. It was a solemn ritual, as it was a time of reflection and communion with the Ancestors. It was a time to invite their continued presence with us. In keeping with the custom of the Musqueam, we did not record or photograph this ceremony.

It was a year between the site dedication ceremony and the sod turning ceremony. During that time, the architects had completed extensive research on the Musqueam shed-style longhouse. They had prepared a pre-design brief, a schematic brief, and created a model

of the longhouse complex for approval. In addition, work had proceeded toward securing the required timber from MacMillan Bloedel, and Heatherbrae Construction was awarded the construction contract.

In December 1990, Larry McFarland, the chief architect, accompanied us on a tour to New Zealand, which I had organized to learn about Maori language immersion programs. We visited several *marae,* which are the meeting places of the Maori people. Larry was particularly interested in the architecture of the meeting houses and how the culture of the Maori was accommodated through these structures.

Sod Turning, 31 May 1991

The sod turning ceremony was attended by several hundred people. Among the special guests were the Elders of the Musqueam Nation and the Honourable Ramon Hnatyshyn, the Governor General of Canada.

Cheryl Banfield, the events co-ordinator of the UBC Development Office, organized the ceremony. A stage, complete with an awning in case of rain, was put up along with three smaller tents. One held the longhouse model and drawings, and the other two were for the food service following the ceremony.

The ceremony began with my introduction of Elder Vince Stogan, who welcomed the guests and gave the

Top: Verna J. Kirkness with Elders Minnie Croft, Vince Stogan, and Simon Baker at sod turning ceremony.

Bottom: Minnie Croft, Simon Baker, David Strangway, Governor General Ramon Hnatyshyn, Vince Stogan, and

Chancellor Leslie Peterson at sod turning ceremony.

Photos: UBC ITServices, Telestudios

27

David Strangway, Vince Stogan, Ramon Hnatyshyn, Minnie Croft, Chancellor Leslie R. Peterson, Verna J. Kirkness, and Eric Denhoff are the official delegation for the sod turning ceremony.
Photo: UBC ITServices, Telestudios

opening prayer. I introduced Chancellor Leslie Peterson, who then conducted the sod turning ceremony. He called on the program speakers, who were His Excellency Governor General Ramon Hnatyshyn, Deputy Minister of Native Affairs Eric Denhoff, Mayor Gordon Campbell, Mr Kenneth Bagshaw, chairman of the university's Board of Governors, and UBC President Dr Strangway. Following their remarks, gold-plated shovels were provided to the Governor General, Elder Vince Stogan, and Ken Bagshaw. In unison they turned the sod, marking the official home of the longhouse.

A naming ceremony followed for Jack Bell. I offered a few remarks: "Your excellencies, Mr Chancellor, Mr President, Elders, honoured guests. The University of British Columbia is situated on the traditional territory of the Musqueam people. We are honoured to have members of the Musqueam Nation with us to confer on Jack Bell a Musqueam name. Elders Dominic Point and Vince Stogan will conduct the naming ceremony."

Elder Dominic Point and Tom Berger draped a blanket on Jack Bell that was woven by Margaret Louis, Musqueam Nation Salish weaver. The name Sty-Wet-Tan was conferred on Jack Bell, the first major donor to give $1 million toward the construction of the longhouse. It was decided that the great hall would be named Sty-Wet-Tan after the newly named Jack Bell. Dominic Point explained:

Sty-Wet-Tan comes from the Musqueam Nation. From the beginning of time, the Musqueam have acknowledged and respected spiritual powers. Sty-Wet-Tan is the west wind spiritual power, which introduces and recognizes the people of the West. The name Sty-Wet-Tan conferred on Dr Jack Bell is most fitting as he has made it possible for the West to host people from all of British Columbia, Canada, and other countries in a Coast Salish longhouse where all can experience the spiritual powers of our Ancestors.

I then introduced the three witnesses who were chosen to speak: Elders Minnie Croft and Chief Simon Baker and the Honourable Emmett Hall. We were very pleased that Emmett Hall could be with us. His Supreme Court judgement in 1973 in the *Calder* case, brought by the Nisga'a people of British Columbia, is the leading judgement affirming Aboriginal rights in Canadian law. The speakers talked in turn about the importance of creating a home-like cultural environment for First Nations students at UBC, and that such a home would attract more First Nations people to pursue further study.

A warrior dance was performed by a group of Musqueam dancers. Grace Mirehouse, assistant director of the Native Education Centre, presented a drum to the First Nations Longhouse. The First Nations House of Learning gave blankets to the Elders present, many of whom were from the Musqueam Nation and seated in the front row. Tom Berger gave the closing address and invited the audience to stay to enjoy the refreshments provided by Toody-Ni-Grill and Catering Company and to view the longhouse model and drawings.

To this day, I am convinced that were it not for the timely gift from Jack Bell, the dream of a longhouse might have been just that – a dream. I believe that it was divine providence that brought him to us at a crucial time. We wanted to build a longhouse. Jack Bell wanted to share his fortune and had a strong sense of compassion for those struggling to make their lives better. We were a perfect match and I am forever indebted to him.

The date 17 March 1989 is very memorable for me. It was the day that Dr Strangway telephoned me to say, "This may be the beginning of your longhouse!" He told me that Jack Bell had invited him for lunch. After they had finished their meal, Mr Bell said to him, "David, if you pay the bill, I will give you this" and handed him a cheque for $1 million, which he said was for First Nations at UBC. Since then, the story of this famous lunch has been recounted many times.

Housepost and Roof-Beam Raising, 17 July 1992

Months of work went into the carving project before the housepost and roof-beam raising ceremony was held. On 18 March 1991, sixteen months prior to the ceremony, a call for submissions was sent to First Nations artists, inviting them to submit renderings if they wished to be considered for the work of carving the two roof beams and four houseposts. A page showing old-style houseposts and beams was sent to the artists, along with sketches of the proposed longhouse. As could be expected, the number and quality of the submissions was remarkable.

Bill McLennan of the Museum of Anthropology at UBC was invited by our Building Committee to take charge of the project. He assessed the submissions to ensure that they met the earthquake shearing and structural standards defined by the architects. This requirement set the depth of cut and the amount of wood that the artists were able to remove to create a finished housepost. The artists selected managed to accommodate these restrictions without compromising the quality of their designs.

The final choice was left to Elders Simon Baker, Minnie Croft, Vince Stogan, and Dominic Point. It was a daunting task to choose from the enthusiastic response to the call for entries. The Elders decided that there should be a range of styles to represent the various traditions of West Coast carvings.

While the selection process was going on, logs for the longhouse were being harvested. The two roof beams were harvested from a forty-four-metre long cedar found in the headwaters of the Sitka Valley, north of the Eve River. Before being carved, the beams were trimmed to twenty-metre lengths with a diameter of almost a metre. The logs that were to be the houseposts were saddled to accommodate the roof beams. The bases of the posts were slotted and bored so that they would sit on 1.2 metre threaded steel rods anchored to concrete pads.

What emerged from these logs is a testament to the artistic ability of each of the carvers. Their contribution to a worthwhile cause will be appreciated for years to come. The carvings were completed in the allotted time and stored in a rented shed on the Musqueam reserve until the great hall of the longhouse was ready for them.

The housepost and roof-beam raising ceremony marked another important milestone in the building of the longhouse. The Elders and Ron Hamilton of the Nuu-chah-nulth Nation, a former UBC graduate, helped guide me in the procedure for an official pole raising ceremony. After Vince Stogan gave the opening prayer and welcomed the guests, the houseposts were unveiled one at a time. As each was uncovered, I introduced its artists, who in turn came to the podium to address the audience. The pride they felt in the work they had done was evident. Their families were present to witness and celebrate their achievement.

The four carved houseposts and two carved roof-beam ends would become the interior of the great hall. What a dramatic sight it was to see the houseposts unveiled, each revealing its own distinct story. There was a great hush over the crowd as the massive roof beams were hoisted in the air by a crane and carefully brought to rest on top of the houseposts. Ron sang a Nuu-chah-nulth song during the raising of the roof beams.

Dressed in full regalia, artists Stan Bevan and Ken McNeil performed a traditional dance around the housepost they had carved. Their uncle, Dempsey Bob, a renowned West Coast artist with whom they had both apprenticed, was present and joined them in the dance. The conclusion of this ceremony meant that the construction of the great hall could now be completed.

Almost every day, I found myself walking over to the site to see what progress was being made. If I had questions or concerns about anything I observed, I would immediately draw these to the attention of Larry McFarland, the architect, and he would quickly

Top: Chief Simon Baker and Verna J. Kirkness give an opening address.
Photo: Larry McFarland Architects

Bottom: The foundations of the great hall can be seen as a roof beam is hoisted onto its houseposts.
Photo: Pam Brown

Facing page: Guests watch as
Don Yeomans' roof beam is
placed atop its houseposts.

Photo: Pam Brown

Below: Susan Point's housepost
is placed on steel rods.

Photo: Larry McFarland Architects

Stan Bevan performs a traditional
Tlingit dance.

Photo: Beverley Berger

Verna Kirkness gets caught up in the process.

Photo: Bill Keay, *Vancouver Sun*

address the matter. I felt so good after the housepost ceremony that the next day, I went over and hugged a pole.

In the eight months between the raising of the houseposts and the longhouse cleansing ceremony in March 1993, all the construction was completed. As well as the longhouse main building with the great hall, a separate building was erected for the library thirty metres away using a contemporary interpretation of a pit house, which was a traditional winter dwelling used by the Interior Salish. In the Chinook trade language, it was also known as a *kekuli* house. It is set into the natural grade at the eastern corner of the site, facilitating access to the main core of the campus.

Adjacent to the library, the dominant feature of the landscape is the waterfall, which begins at road height by the pit house. The concrete waterfall was textured to represent sedimentary rock formation over which water flows into a river. The rocks used for the riverbed were quarried in Coquitlam. The boulders and pebbles extend underneath the boardwalk alongside the administrative offices leading to the great hall. The waterfall was Chief Simon Baker's idea. He explained, "Water is the most important thing in our lives. I was born and raised by the river. Our old people used to say, 'Water is your best friend.' They would tell us to go and swim even when we were just toddlers. Mother Earth gave us water. They would ask us, 'Where did the water come from?'

Below, Xwi7xwa Library. The posts outside are part of the pit house structure.

Photo: UBC ITServices, Telestudios

Right, pit house poles seen from below.

Photo: Jack G.M. Wong

Far right, waterfall.

Photo: George Vaitkunas

It comes from the mountains, the snow. 'Where did the water go?' It went out to the sea. It goes in a cycle. If we didn't have water we would perish. These teachings gave me the idea to have a waterfall."

Longhouse Cleansing, 13 March 1993

A gathering was held to cleanse and bless the newly constructed longhouse. Elders Vince and Edna Stogan of the Musqueam Nation opened the ceremony with prayer and with the offering of food and drink to cleanse the building. This was to honour and welcome the Ancestors to the longhouse. Vince explained, "What we are doing today is our way of welcoming you folks to this place, to get ready for the important work which will begin in the First Nations Longhouse. We want to do it in a proper way so that we honour the Ancestors of this place, so we cleanse it and welcome them to this building which will be for everyone's use."

Other Nations performed appropriate ceremonies. A sweetgrass ceremony was led by Thomas Little, an Oji/Cree theology student from Island Lake, Manitoba: "It gives us the opportunity to commune with the spirits of this place and of this land ... We have come to be with one another, to bring under one roof a method of teaching ... that will cover all the nations of this, our Mother Earth ... The Eagle Feather, the strongest spiritual guide that I have, I brought with me. Upon this feather I have tried to acknowledge all the people of the earth. Let us be with them in spirit."

Members of the Kwagiulth Nation, among them Elders Alfred and Joan Scow, danced in full regalia, spreading eagle down around the perimeter of the longhouse, while Elder Henry Seaweed called on the spirits to welcome people to the building and to ensure the peaceful use of the premises.

Inside the longhouse, Robert Davidson and the Rainbow Creek Dancers sang songs of the Haida Nation to honour the occasion. The ceremony concluded with a friendship dance led by Chief Simon Baker. Finally, having fully prepared the longhouse for our entry, we moved into the building on 13 March 1993.

The Artists

Lyle Wilson

Lyle Wilson, internationally renowned Haisla artist, carved the two-sided housepost that stands at the southeast entrance to Sty-Wet-Tan, the great hall. He also created the adzed finish for the ceremonial door.

He was previously commissioned to produce two carvings for Canada's exhibit at Expo '92 in Barcelona, Spain. These are just two of the many works that

The ceremonial door carved by Lyle Wilson depicts an Eagle.
Photo: The Media Group, Woodward Instructional Resources Centre, UBC

Facing page: Two views of the Beaver and Eagle Housepost; overall view, left, and detail, right.
Photos: George Vaitkunas

have earned him international acclaim. In 1987, Lyle was a project co-ordinator in the creation of five big-houses and a longhouse from the Northwest Coast that were installed in the grand hall of the new Canadian Museum of Civilization in Hull, Quebec. His first artistic influence was his uncle, Sam Robinson. Lyle began to pursue art as a profession while attending UBC, where he was enrolled in art education. He later graduated from the Emily Carr College of Art and Design.

The Beaver and Eagle Housepost

The Beaver and the Eagle symbolize the clan crests of Lyle Wilson's parents in Kitamaat village. Both figures are represented on the housepost he carved, on opposite sides. Lyle explains, "The housepost is a traditional concept. Usually only the front would be seen. However, the design of this one is 360 degrees. I divided the pole into two halves. The middle part is a representation of a potlatch pole. My family clan crests are shown. The Beaver is my mother's and grandmother's clan crest; the Eagle is my father's. I want to do a really nice job as I went to UBC for five years. This pole has sentiment to it."

The Beaver, facing out toward the window, has the arms and legs of a person and the face or mask of a stylized beaver. This face mask is encircled by a braided cedar rope, and an oval wooden band in turn encircles the rope. Inlaid on the flat surface of the oval are rays alternately shining out from the face and running parallel to the cedar rope. The hands of the figure reach out to touch the throat. The legs are bent as if in a dance stance. There is another face in the belly of the masked figure and two small faces on the backs of the hands. Inlaid octagons appear like buttons in a row down the chest front.

The Eagle, facing toward the interior of the great hall, is almost identical in form and size to the Beaver

but with an Eagle face mask. Faces emerge from the
belly and backs of the hands. The Eagle has the legs of
a human and hands that reach up to the throat. A
cedar rope encircles the face mask and the sun ray base
surrounds the rope and the face. The buttons down
the front are not octagons but circles.

This beautifully carved housepost is unpainted, but
the eyes, hand masks, circles, and octagons are of inlaid
yellow cedar. At the unveiling of the houseposts on
17 July 1992, Lyle proudly stated, "This longhouse will
be here for all future generations of learners."

Stan Bevan and Ken McNeil

Stan Bevan is Tahltan-Tlingit-Tsimshian and Ken
McNeil is Tahltan-Tlingit-Nisg̲a'a. Their Raven house-
post stands at the northeast corner of Sty-Wet-Tan.
Raven is portrayed as the one who brings knowledge.

Stan Bevan became interested in the arts and carving
at an early age through the influence of his uncle,
Dempsey Bob. He completed a six-month program at
the famous K'san School of Northwest Coast Indian
Art in Hazelton, British Columbia. Two years later, he
became an apprentice to Dempsey Bob, the well-
known Tlingit master artist. The Tlingit social system
is matrilineal, and it is customary for an uncle to train
his sister's sons. Stan worked on several of Dempsey

Stan Bevan and Ken McNeil.
Photo: Pam Brown

Bob's major commissions, including a ten-metre totem pole in Ketchikan, Alaska, before working on his own projects. He has been included in many exhibitions documenting Northwest Coast art.

Stan Bevan's cousin, Ken McNeil, has also been influenced by their uncle, Dempsey Bob. He began carving at the age of fourteen, apprenticed with his uncle, and began to practise his own art full time in 1987. The transition from apprentice to artist was assisted by the opportunity to work on two of Dempsey's notable commissions. The first was a three-dimensional panel carved in the round for the entrance hall to the Ridley Coal Terminal, outside Prince Rupert. The sculpture also bears Ken's signature for his overall artistic contribution. The second was a large sculpted panel mounted outside the terminal. These major projects offered valuable experience in contractual agreements, deadlines, and other aspects of

the art business. In a remarkably short period, Ken has earned the respect of the international audience addressing Northwest Coast art. He has had a number of exhibitions.

Man and Raven Housepost

A human figure at the top of the carving has black brows and eyes and reddish brown inner lips and nostrils. The figure is smiling with teeth showing. The hands, which are by the sides of the body, are holding the wings of Raven, who is looking up into the human's face. Raven's beak is resting in intimate and trusting repose under the chin of the human. Raven's eyes and wings are black. His mouth, nostrils, and one wing on each side are reddish brown.

From Raven's back a sharp-nosed human face – the spirit within Raven – is smiling and looking out. The human's hands and feet protrude from under the Raven's wing in a kneeling position.

One of the intriguing aspects of the carving is the unity within the three figures of the carving. The human and Raven resting flat against it seem like two forms of the same person, with the third peeking out from the back of the Raven. They seem attached by more than the post they emerge from, as if these are three faces of one person.

Ken McNeil.

Photo: Bill McLennan, Museum of Anthropology

Facing page: Two views of Man and Raven Housepost; detail, left, and overall view, right.

Photos: George Vaitkunas

43

Walter Harris speaks about the housepost that he carved with Rodney Harris.
Photo: Beverley Berger

Rodney Harris, son of Walter Harris, speaks at the housepost raising ceremony.
Photo: Beverley Berger

Facing page: Two views of Wolf and Wolf Pup Housepost; overall view, left, and detail, right.
Photos: George Vaitkunas

Chief Walter Harris and Rodney Harris

Chief Walter Harris and his son, Rodney, are Gitxsan artists from Kispiox. Walter is a well-known carver who works in wood, stone, gold, silver, metal, and silkscreening. He became interested in Northwest Coast art forms while helping in the construction of the K'san Village in the 1960s. At the K'san School of Northwest Coast Indian Art, he was named senior instructor of wood sculpture, a position he held for many years. His work has found its way to all parts of the world and includes a high-relief stone sculpture located above the entry to the House of Commons in Ottawa, wall-sized panel murals in the Canadian embassy in Paris, and a twelve-metre pole – located in Golden Gate Park in San Francisco – honouring America's bicentennial. He was also one of the carvers of the doors of the Museum of Anthropology at the University of British Columbia.

Rodney Harris graduated from Hazelton Secondary School in 1979. He entered the K'san School in 1982. He also developed his artistic skills by working with his father. Since 1989, he has devoted himself full time to his carving.

The Harrises carved the housepost situated at the northwest corner of Sty-Wet-Tan. The housepost has three human figures facing inward toward the great hall, and a wolf holding a pup. The Wolf is Rodney's mother's crest. Because the Gitxsan is a matrilineal society, Rodney will inherit his mother's crest and clan. At the housepost unveiling, Doreen Jensen, spokesperson for Chief Walter Harris, remarked, "The Wolf is the crest of Sadie Harris, wife to Walter and mother to Rod. The Gitxsan are a matrilineal people. The mothers and grandmothers are very responsible for the early ... and continuing education of our young people. Because this housepost stands on Musqueam territory, we consider that [it] is an ambassador from the Gitxsan Fireweed tribe in northern BC. The housepost also represents the fact that we have a teacher from the Wolf clan."

Wolf and Wolf Pup Housepost

Three human figures at the top of the housepost represent the students who will come here to learn. Standing tall, one faces left, one faces forward, one faces right.

The stylized wolf figure below has a human quality in that it is standing upright holding a young pup in its hands. The hands have the look of claws on extended human fingers. The feet look like human feet. The head looks like a stylized ceremonial mask.

The pup is more realistic looking. Its head, ears, face, snout, body shape, paws, and tail are naturalistic, more like the wolf with which we are familiar.

Susan Point

Susan Point, Coast Salish artist, is a carver, printmaker, and jeweller from Musqueam. Jack Leyland, Bill Watson, and John Livingstone taught her the technical skills of jewellery making, screen printing, and wood carving, as she set about to revive the ancient principles of Coast Salish two-dimensional design. Susan carved the welcome figure and the spindle whorl that stand at the new Vancouver Airport. She also carved the housepost that stands at the southwest entrance to Sty-Wet-Tan. It was her first major wood carving "in the round."

Raven with Spindle Whorl Housepost

Raven, the Trickster, a mythological character who was present at the creation, faces toward the hall with gleaming eyes of copper, denoting the wealth and the nobility of the coastal people. His eyes protrude from stylized eye sockets that are stained reddish brown, as are the inside of his beak and three crescent shapes on his front. Two dark, pointed crescents arch over the eyes, giving Raven the transformational look of another form or of a mask to be worn at ceremonies.

Raven has two rows of wing feathers carved gracefully around the pole, with tail feathers extending downward at the back. He seems to hold his wings close like a blanket to keep warm, the way grandmothers sit at the winter potlatches. His beak is mortised on, giving Raven's face more dimension. His feet rest on a spindle whorl, the symbol of the powerful place of women in Northwest culture.

The disk-shaped spindle whorl, with a hole in the centre, was traditionally used by Coast Salish women to spin and ply goat or dog wool into yarn for weaving. It is said that a woman's wealth was judged by the number of wool-bearing dogs she owned. The spindle whorl in the carving is a large circle with a Raven design in black and a reddish brown and natural cedar background. Raven is looking up to the left with wings outspread as if to fly away. Inside his wings, two large eyes look out at the viewer, revealing the human spirit that lives within.

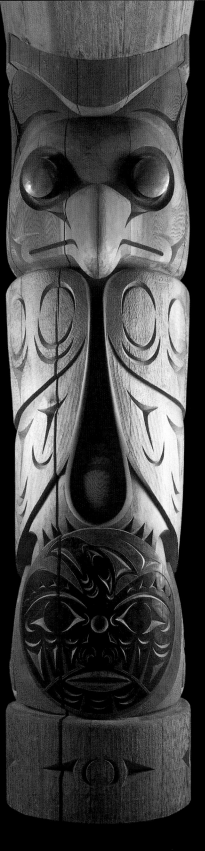

Don Yeomans carves one of the longhouse roof beam ends.

Photo: Bill McLennan, Museum of Anthropology

Facing page, photo: Steven Evans

Don Yeomans

Don Yeomans, a Haida/Métis artist, started at the age of eleven to carve with his aunt, Freda Diesing. In 1976, at eighteen, he came to Vancouver to enroll in a fine arts program at Langara College. There he met instructor Bud Mintz, who became instrumental in encouraging the development of his career as an artist. In 1978, he participated in the carving of four Haida houseposts for the village of Old Massett. The project involved seven other apprentices and was supervised by his childhood idol, Haida artist Robert Davidson. In 1983, he accepted a teaching position in Victoria, teaching basic design and carving in the public school system. In 1986, Don went to work with the famous Haida artist Bill Reid on a totem pole commission. He works in wood and precious metals, producing embossed and cast works. As well, he creates limited edition prints, most of them serigraphs. He carved the ends of the two roof beams in Sty-Wet-Tan. The two beams, each weighing 4,500 kilograms, represent Sea Lion and Killer Whale.

Bradley Hunt

Bradley Hunt is a carver and former schoolteacher from the Heiltsuk Nation at Waglisla (Bella Bella). He began to carve as a young boy and later attended the Vancouver School of Art (now Emily Carr College of Art and Design) and the University of British Columbia. He notes, "The honoured traditions of Heiltsuk artistry had all but disappeared from my village of Waglisla in the early days of European contact, when the intricate work was dismissed as a simple craft of a primitive culture." By reading about and studying past generations of his people, he has been successful in bringing Heiltsuk culture back into his life. Bradley works primarily with yellow and red cedar. He has been commissioned to carve a variety of pieces, including masks, totem poles, and talking sticks. Many of his masks have been worn for dances in traditional potlatch ceremonies.

Bradley carved the pair of doors that open between the great hall and the other parts of the longhouse. The doors show a split salmon with human figures both inside the fish and at the base of the image. The close relationship between people and fish is central to his design. The same salmon and human images are also painted on the reverse side of the carved doors. Two more uncarved sliding cedar doors were also installed to give privacy between the great hall and the foyer when events required it. The Native Fishing Association donated $25,000 for the four large cedar doors in Sty-Wet-Tan.

The Path That Led to the Longhouse

It had taken over four years to complete the First Nations Longhouse. Although the time was short, a great deal had gone into it. I thought of how the project began.

In 1988, as Director of the First Nations House of Learning, I was officially informed of the plan to demolish the wartime huts that housed our First Nations programs. One of the NITEP huts had already been demolished. Knowing that we would eventually have to be relocated, I began to pursue one of the objectives of the First Nations House of Learning, which was to establish a physical facility on campus to enhance access and support services for First Nations students. There was a consensus among the students, the Elders, the staff, and the Advisory Committee members that we should explore this possibility.

In the fall of 1988, I held a meeting with the students and staff to brainstorm about a longhouse. Many of the ideas presented that day were later incorporated

Facing page: Doors carved by Bradley Hunt.
Photo: George Vaitkunas

51

into the design. In January 1989, I convened the first full meeting of Elders, staff, and students to talk about the concept of a longhouse on campus. In early March, a second meeting was convened to discuss the purpose of the longhouse and what we would like to see included in the building. The enthusiasm of people at that meeting was an indication of the excitement felt at the prospect of having such a facility. The wish list included a lounge, a computer room, a great hall, a kitchen, a library, a daycare, a carving room, a dark room for developing photographs, a studio for making silver and gold jewellery, and office space to house the various First Nations programs.

On 17 March 1989, Jack Bell donated $1 million for First Nations at UBC. Encouraged, I immediately initiated meetings with various groups to get opinions about the best use of the money. I met the First Nations House of Learning Advisory Committee and the Native Indian Education Advisory Committee, and called a meeting of students, staff, and faculty. A unanimous decision was made to put the money toward the construction of a longhouse. The money could have gone toward scholarships and bursaries, but we all agreed that we needed our home away from home. The First Nations House of Learning Advisory Committee officially agreed to designate the Jack Bell donation for the construction

of a longhouse on 12 May 1989. This recommendation went forward to the President's Office. Once approval was received, we proceeded with our planning.

Jack Bell was pivotal to realizing our dream, as his donation triggered our participation in a university fundraising campaign. The UBC World of Opportunity Campaign was already under way prior to this donation, and the longhouse project had not been included. Once we had $1 million, however, our project became part of the campaign and our funds immediately doubled to $2 million, as the province had agreed to match funds for capital projects as part of this campaign.

To spearhead the project, I established and chaired a building committee of Elders, students, staff, and faculty to oversee the project. The committee consisted of Elders Simon Baker, Minnie Croft, Vince Stogan, Joan Scow, Alfred Scow, students Philip Hogan and Alfie Waugh, fundraising co-ordinator Catherine Newlands from the Development Office, director of the Native Law Program Steven Point, and on-campus NITEP co-ordinator Roger Smith. Victor Jim, a teacher from Moricetown, and Len Marchand, a senator in Parliament, were corresponding members.

Though the first official meeting of the Building Committee took place on 5 October 1989, many meetings were held right from the beginning of the project and were open to students, staff, and any other interested persons, a practice that continued throughout the project. The Elders played a prominent role from the outset. Their insight, guidance, and encouragement were a constant and sustaining force in the project.

I remember what fun it was to be with the Elders. I often picked them up for our meetings because I enjoyed hearing their humorous stories and the way they joked with one another. During the times when we were facing difficult challenges, they stood firm in their belief that our dream would come true. They were always there to give me confidence and to boost my spirit.

The university gave us considerable freedom in advancing the project. This enabled us, the First Nations people at UBC, to determine and oversee every stage of the building of the longhouse. We were the visionaries behind the whole process.

The first major decision we had to make was to choose an architect. The university shortlisted the candidates to three. Each of these was interviewed at least twice by our Building Committee before we made a final selection. We chose Larry McFarland Architects for two main reasons. First, the company had built a longhouse at Prince Rupert, which Larry McFarland invited us to visit. Larry, Chief Simon Baker, and I went

for the day. We were impressed with the building and with the respect with which Larry treated us. Second, he was clearly a person who would understand us and be willing to take direction from our committee, as we wanted the building to reflect our vision. We also met other people in his firm who would be working on the project. With that, we recommended to the university that the company be awarded the contract.

Following the appointment on 31 October 1989, we immediately scheduled a series of meetings to acquaint Larry McFarland with what we had discussed at previous meetings about the purpose and function of the longhouse and to discuss process, scheduling, site, and funding.

Larry presented a plan for how we might make decisions about the building in a systematic manner through a series of workshops. This would ensure the maximum participation of all the stakeholders. The workshops would be held biweekly in the student lounge of the NITEP hut. The series of meetings about the building site illustrates the process and outcome of the workshops. In this series of workshops, we considered where the longhouse should be located. Led by one or more of Larry McFarland's architectural team, we discussed a number of issues. First, we addressed the functional adjacencies of the longhouse to the

David Wilkinson of Larry McFarland Architects takes notes as Chief Simon Baker speaks at a planning workshop.

Photo: Larry McFarland Architects

academic core, to parking facilities, to pedestrian access, to public transit, to vehicular access, and to public facilities. This was followed by a discussion of the character that we wanted the longhouse to portray on campus. We talked about its visibility, the ambiance of the site, the neighbourhood, safety of the environment to the users, and its prestige in terms of location. Finally, we considered site development implications. We reviewed the servicing costs (electricity, water, sewer), control of the site in the sense of the building establishing a presence without being dominated by the surrounding built environment, the impact on the existing natural environment, and how favourable the area was for a building.

During each workshop, responses to the questions were recorded on flip charts. The architects would then review all the comments and bring a summary to the following session before we moved on to a further topic. Using a rating of factors scale, we determined the kind of site most favoured. We then visited the five possible sites we had to choose from and concluded this exercise unanimously in favour of the West Mall site as being the ideal location.

To encourage and enable students to attend, we scheduled the workshops to begin at 12:30 p.m. Sometimes we provided soup and sandwiches or chili, and at other times it was a potluck event. Many students would have to leave for class again at 1:20 p.m., but those who could stay or join us at any time during the usual two-hour workshop did so. The workshops were usually very well attended. Along with an opening prayer, one of the Elders often had a message of encouragement and some comment about the importance of the project. Regardless of the number who were still in attendance at the end of each workshop, we formed a circle, joined hands to keep our circle strong, and closed with a prayer.

The workshops were held throughout January and February 1990, covering four major areas: identity, function, site, and image. It was a very effective process

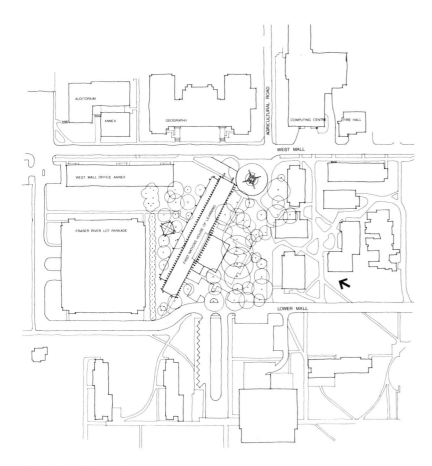

The site plan of the longhouse grounds shows the numerous trees that the architects managed to preserve.

Photo: Larry McFarland Architects

Summary of the design objectives from the workshop on image.

Photo: Larry McFarland Architects

'LONGHOUSE' IS JUST A NAME. —CHIEF SIMON BAKER	WATER THE MOST IMPORTANT ELEMENT.	A GATHERING PLACE. A SPIRITUAL PLACE.	'WELCOMING'
EXPRESS **INTEGRATION WITH THE LANDSCAPE** RESPECT FOR THE LAND.	**EXCITEMENT** OF THE NATURAL **PROPERTIES** OF **MATERIALS**	EXPRESS **CONTROL** OVER **CHANGE**.	"HOME AWAY FROM HOME" REFLECTS A GENERAL DESIRE FOR **ATMOSPHERE** AND **SCALE**
THE MEDICINE WHEEL USE AS A **SYMBOL** OF THE **HOLISTIC** APPROACH A POWERFUL SYMBOL	: **EVOKE** THE **CYCLES** OF THE **SEASONS** & **CONTINUITY** OF LIFE ITSELF	"**WITNESSING**"	THE ARCHITECTURE OF THE **CAMPUS** EXPRESSES A **FORMALITY** AND A **HIERARCHY**.
FORMALITY OF **EVENTS** ....COEXISTING WITH DAILY **INFORMALITY**.	• **COMMUNITY** • **SPIRITUALITY** • **STRENGTH** • **CEREMONY**	: A **SPACE FOR REFLECTION** ↓ SPIRIT RENEWAL	: **LIVING**, BREATHING ENTITY THAT **GROWS** & FLOWS FROM **INSIDE OUT**
EXPRESS **SIGNIFICANCE OF TRADITION** AMIDST **CHANGE** AND CULTURAL **SURVIVAL**	CIRCLE	MINIMIZE THE **VISIBLE** USE OF **CONCRETE**	• A "**HOME**" AWAY '**FROM HOME**'
USE OF **MATERIALS** DOES NOT NEED TO BE CONSTRAINED BY **HISTORIC TECHNOLOGY**.	THE **PLACE** MUST NOT BE **SUBJUGATED** BY THE **BUILDING**.	**IMAGE** SHOULD EXPRESS THE **FACT** THAT WE ARE ON **SALISH** LAND.	MEDICINE WHEEL DIRECTIONS COLOURS ANIMAL HELPERS FOOD PLACES
LONGHOUSE: AN EXAMPLE OF **LIFE** & BY DEFINITION THERE ARE **PRIVATE** & **PUBLIC** ASPECTS	THE BUILDING(S) MUST LOOK AND FEEL **COMFORTABLE** TO **FIRST PEOPLES**	NOTION OF BUILDINGS AS **INSTRUCTIONAL** BY WAY OF ITS **COMPONENTS** AND **DETAILS**	CHANGING **FUNCTION** MEANS CHANGING **FORM**.

as it enabled all of us to contribute our thoughts on these various aspects.

Another very important event in the process of building the longhouse was the meeting with the Musqueam Band Council on 17 April 1990. I made an appointment with Chief Wendy Grant of the Musqueam Nation to discuss the longhouse project with her and the Council. The architect, the Elders, and others attended the meeting. The purpose was to inform the Council of our intention to build a longhouse at UBC, as the university is situated on the traditional territory of the Musqueam Nation. I thought it was only proper to do this even though we had a Musqueam Elder, Vince Stogan, on our committee.

We made our presentation, outlining to the Chief and Council what we proposed to do and why a longhouse on campus was needed. After we had finished, we were asked if the Council could meet *in camera* for a few minutes. When we rejoined the Council, we were told that they liked our idea but had only one request to make. They asked if we could use a traditional Musqueam shed-style design. They were unable to give us drawings of a traditional Musqueam longhouse so it was necessary for the architects to research this area. The Council designated one of its members, Councillor Joe Becker, to act as the liaison until the appropriate model was identified. Through Joe Becker and Elder Vince Stogan, we were able to keep the Musqueam Council informed of our progress.

CONSTRUCTION

The longhouse is constructed primarily of cedar. MacMillan Bloedel supplied the carefully selected logs from their inventory at Port Alberni, Port McNeill, Kelsey Bay, and Squamish. Timber was also purchased from Weldwood Company and from Canadian Forest Products. The logs were barged, boomed, and trucked to Heatherbrae's processing site near Gibsons Landing, where they were milled to a constant diameter. The logs intended for columns and beams had their connection details cut into them at this stage. As well, many of the logs were hewn for the siding of the building.

The harvesting and processing of the logs took approximately a year, and the actual construction of the longhouse took fifteen months. At any given time, nearly twenty people were working on the site and at other times as many as thirty. Included among them were drywall finishers, electricians, glaziers, and labourers, to name a few. These people took pride in the realization of the vision.

Falling and inspection of large-diameter cedar logs at the Eve River Logging Division of MacMillan Bloedel was followed by fabrication at the Heatherbrae Construction yard. The logs were milled to the desired diameter and lengths were cut with notches and splines.

Photos: Larry McFarland Architects

The longhouse under
construction.

Facing page: The longhouse
roof resembles the wings of a
bird in flight.

Copper was chosen as the roofing material because of its traditional value to the coastal people. The copper roofing was made in France, by one of only two manufacturers in the world. The roof system was made up of two layers of asphalt-impregnated fibreglass sheets. The base sheet was stapled to the plywood roof sheathing and laid so that each successive layer overlapped the previous one and was "torched on" where the upper layer covered the nails of the lower level. The top sheet had the copper layer bonded to it and was then installed in the same manner as the base sheet.

The longhouse roof resembles the wings of a bird in flight. One copper wing sweeps toward the past, to our cultures that have existed for many thousands of years, and the other wing sweeps toward the future, signifying the blend of new knowledge to our cultures.

The exterior of the great hall is finished with rough-hewn cedar hung horizontally. The placement of the siding is representative of Salish architecture, and the copper wire that encircles the lashing posts is intended to symbolize cedar rope. The interior of the great hall is 270 square metres. This multipurpose room can accommodate up to 400 people. It is the focal point of the longhouse, used for graduation ceremonies, conferences, meetings, guest lectures, feasts, and other special events and social functions.

The exterior of the great hall is finished with rough-hewn cedar hung horizontally. Copper wire encircles the posts.

Photo: Malak

Inside the longhouse, roughly hewn cedar is hung to represent Northwest Coast First Nations architecture. A two-storey curtain wall in the reception area is an interpretation of the traditional Coast Salish longhouse wall system. The housefront behind the reception desk is also in the Northwest Coast style, as can be seen in the gabled configuration, with fascia beams forming the slope and providing weather protection to vertical cedar planks of random width.

The building also features many of the elements on our original wish list. The student computer room is designed to accommodate at least ten computer work stations and is accessible to students twenty-four hours a day. The Living Cultures Room serves as an artists' studio for small carving projects, craft activities, storage of ceremonial material, and Elders' cultural workshops. The combined staff and student lounge has a kitchenette and provides a friendly meeting place for everyone to share conversation, food, and activities. The Elders' Room is adjacent to the staff and student lounge. It is designed for the use of Elders visiting the longhouse and for Elders-in-Residence sessions with students, and it can accommodate up to ten people. As well as coffee tables and comfortable chairs, it contains a set of small tables and chairs for children to use.

A large seminar room is adjacent to X̲wi7x̲wa Library.

The reception area has a Northwest Coast housefront replica behind the front desk.
Photo: Larry McFarland Architects

The student computer room is open twenty-four hours a day.
Photo: Bentley Wong

Top: The boardroom is usually heavily booked.

Centre: X̱wi7x̱wa Library houses a large collection of First Nations material.

Bottom: The Elders' Room is used for Elders' visits and Elders-in-Residence programs.

Photos: Bentley Wong

It can hold thirty to forty people for First Nations courses, seminars, symposia, and special event classes. As well as the longhouse administrative offices, the building houses a boardroom and an office for the First Nations student associations.

The architects and the Longhouse Building Committee wanted to honour a traditional architectural style by basing the X̱wi7x̱wa Library structure on the Interior Salish pit house. Pit houses were winter homes built around a circular pit, approximately a metre deep, with an average diameter of 3.6 metres. The house could accommodate up to thirty people. Pit house shape and construction varied throughout the BC Plateau region, but all used poles as the framework and then a webbing of poles lashed in concentric circles from pit to smokehole, which supported a snug layer of smaller poles. A covering of materials such as bark, earth, grass, and pine needles completed the roof structure. A central fire heated the pit house. Usually, a large cedar post was notched and served as a ladder for entering and leaving the pit house. An opening in the roof structure served the dual purpose of being an entrance and smokehole.

A pit house-style cedar log framework majestically greets people on the West Mall side of the longhouse location. The X̱wi7x̱wa Library is circular and reminds us of the pit house coziness, even though the modern material of concrete and glass are used. The library is 198 square metres and contains two offices, a large collections area with reading and study tables, networked computer stations, and an archives room.

The Sacred Circle has a separate location on the grounds, in a direct line to the great hall. It is available to all who need spiritual sanctuary and can be used as a quiet retreat for rest and reflection. The circular structure has a firepit for ceremonial purposes. Roughly twenty-five people can use it at any one time.

The childcare centre was not built until after the longhouse was officially opened. I secured capital funding from the Ministry of Advanced Education for this purpose. The Longhouse Building Committee worked with Peter Turje, a specialist in childcare centre design, and an associate of Larry McFarland Architects. They provided planning guidelines for the physical facility and began the licensing discussions with the appropriate licensing department.

The childcare centre facility was completed by late 1993, but we didn't have sufficient funding to develop the outdoor area into a playground. Jo-ann Archibald took over the process, and funds to finish and equip the playground were acquired from the Vancouver Foundation, the BC Aboriginal Wellness Program, and

The Sacred Circle is available to all who need spiritual sanctuary.
Photo: George Vaitkunas

later, Aboriginal Head Start, Health Canada. Following discussions with the Longhouse Childcare Centre Planning Committee and in consultation with Peter Turje, landscape architect Robert Degros prepared plans for the playground. The longhouse group wanted to ensure that the children had a natural looking environment in which to play and learn. A huge climbing stump, smaller play stumps and logs, rocks of varying sizes, a sand play area, a stone story circle, two cedar play houses, a small vegetable planting area, two outside deck play areas, berry plants, and various trees make up the playground. The centre did not officially open until March 1995 because of the delays in getting funding and development permits for the playground.

Fundraising

I remember well the first donation ever made for the building of our longhouse. At one of our very early meetings with students, Elders, and staff, Albert Johnson, one of the NITEP students, handed me a five-dollar bill. We smiled at the gesture, believing deep in our hearts that the longhouse would some day be a reality. Shortly thereafter, at another meeting, Chief Simon Baker appeared with what he called a money tree. He pinned his donation to the tree and urged us to do the same. Simon never failed to take advantage of every opportunity to tell people about the longhouse project and to appeal for donations. He was often asked to speak or entertain at First Nations meetings or conferences. On these occasions, he always had some scheme up his sleeve to get some money for us.

I recall another occasion, when Elder Minnie Croft and I were on our way to tell the Gitxsan people in Hazelton about our longhouse project. Before going to the meeting, we stopped at the NITEP Centre in Hazelton to say hello to the students. We told them we were on our way to a meeting, hoping to get support for the longhouse. We had some panels with us showing sketches of how the longhouse might look. The students were very excited about the project, seeing in it the potential for themselves, as they would be on campus at UBC for their last two years of teacher education. A few months later, I received a cheque for $1,000 from the Hazelton NITEP students. They had raised the money through a variety of functions.

What fun we had with our telephone fundraising effort. At the Development Office, several telephones were made available to us for three evenings. A number of students and staff had volunteered to telephone the UBC First Nations graduates to solicit their support. We each had a huge list of people to call. It was wonderful to talk to these former graduates, to touch base with them and tell them of the project. Invariably, much other information was exchanged. How is the teaching going? How many children do you have now? You got married! How is life on the campus? I'm thinking of returning next year to do a master's degree.

The news of our project got around. I was surprised one day to get a telephone call from a Maori friend from New Zealand who was in Canada with the Kahurangi Maori Dance Company. From their Calgary base, the troupe offered to come to Vancouver to put on a show for us, to raise money for the longhouse. We had a full house at the Vancouver Indian Centre that evening and were able to add to our fund.

These informal personal acts of support from our people were very meaningful to us, helping to keep our dream alive. There was also a large, more formal machinery at work within the university to raise funds for the longhouse.

The Development Office of the University of British Columbia had the important job of raising funds for the university's priorities. In 1989, UBC launched its World of Opportunity Campaign to raise funds for buildings, equipment, chairs, professorships, and student aid, with a focus on capital projects. The campaign was launched under the leadership of Vice President of External Affairs Dr Peter Ufford. The provincial government made a commitment to match donations raised from the private sector for up to $90 million. When the campaign ended in 1993, a total of $262 million had been raised, including the matching grant.

As the longhouse project was part of the World of Opportunity Campaign, whatever money was raised was matched. The First Nations Longhouse initial budget came in at $4.9 million. By the time it was completed, the costs had risen to $5.3 million.

The Development Office assigned an officer to the longhouse project. It was her job to assist me, as the Director of the First Nations House of Learning, in identifying potential donors and developing a strategy for fundraising. I had the good fortune of working with Catherine Newlands, Rosemary Ogilve, and Pamela Miles in turn over the course of the four years. They had a sincere interest in the project and worked enthusiastically to meet the challenge of raising the money required.

Working closely with the development officer, I prepared a prospective list of donors, prioritized the list, and waited while the necessary research was completed by the Development Office and the President's Office. This was a very well-orchestrated fundraising campaign, with clear procedures to be followed in seeking out particular donors.

One of the early lessons I learned as I began to fundraise was that I should concentrate my efforts on obtaining large donations, in $1 million range. It was difficult for me, at first, to conceive of that amount but before long, the figure just rolled off my tongue.

Initially, my priority was to solicit funds from First Nations tribal and band councils. I was excited about their involvement. I did eventually launch a campaign directed at First Nations but first I assisted in seeking out large donations. I did not have contacts among people who could give a very generous gift but I was able to provide the information required by the potential donors through meetings or at luncheons, organized by the Development Office. I also did several radio and television interviews. We were fortunate in receiving three large gifts, which when matched by the provincial government's dollars contributed substantially to meeting the cost of the project.

For my fundraising campaign with the First Nations tribal and band councils in the province, I prepared a twenty-page booklet entitled "The First Nations Longhouse at the University of British Columbia." The booklet outlined the purpose of the longhouse and described the student, academic, and administrative services it would provide. I got on the agenda of a number of tribal council meetings around the province to make presentations. Whenever possible, one of the Elders accompanied me. We received a number of donations through this effort.

The President's Office played a very active part in fundraising for the longhouse. President Dr Strangway, Vice President Academic and Provost Dr Birch, and Vice President of External Affairs Dr Peter Ufford all gave the highest priority to securing funds from the federal and provincial government departments, from the private sector, from churches, and from corporations. As Pam Miles, the development officer noted, "It was a very emotional and compassionate project for everyone involved."

It might appear that getting the money for the longhouse was an easy task, but it was not. There were times when I wondered if we could keep the project going. At one point, the project was suspended for a short time because of the question of money. There was always the threat that we might have to scale down our plan. What would we give up? Everything we had planned was integral to making our new home complete. Having a daycare meant that we would have children and their parents, who were our students, in our home. Along with our Elders, we would then have our extended family present in the longhouse. Could we give up our Sacred Circle? It was to be our spiritual sanctuary, a place where we could commune with our higher power, hold ceremonies, or conduct healing circles. I remember thinking what a difficult choice it would be for us to leave out part of our plan. I believe the Creator heard our prayers and the money came in.

Moving into the Longhouse, 15 March 1993

This was an exciting day as we moved from our huts into the new longhouse, our brand new home away from home. Much of the furniture was new and was selected by the staff and students. Some was brought over from the huts. The university took care of the move. It was a day to remember! Larry had a special desk made for me from parts of the big logs used in construction, and the desk top was made of glass. It was an original. All the offices were the same size, a decision I made early on to avoid favouring hierarchy. While most had an outside view, of necessity several had to face inward.

Oh, that smell of cedar was so pleasant! It was an exciting day for us. None of the labour pains associated with the four years of work even entered my mind. All I could think was, "It's done, finished. We are in our new home." Not even a ticket for parking in a restricted area in our new location could dampen my spirits. We had created a dream. Now we could begin to live that dream.

The purpose of the longhouse is to:

· serve as a First Nations community on campus

· serve as a "home away from home," where First Nations students can study and learn in surroundings that reflect their heritage and culture

· unite, under one roof, access and support services that were previously housed in several locations across the UBC campus

· provide a meeting place for people engaged in a multitude of activities

· enable First Nations people to share their knowledge and cultures with each other

· enable First Nations people to share their knowledge and cultures with the general university community and with the larger society.

The People

MANY PEOPLE CONTRIBUTED to the dream of having a longhouse on the campus of the University of British Columbia. It was their vision, their commitment, and their hard work that made it all happen. Among them were the First Nations Elders, students, and staff who took an active interest over the four years it took for the longhouse to be completed. It could not have been done without the university officials who believed in the concept and made it a priority. It could not have been done without the generous contribution of the many donors.

The Elders

Elder Minnie Croft is Haida, from the House of Skedans in Haida Gwaii. The First Nations Longhouse Committee was fortunate to have this insightful, generous woman as one of the guiding forces in the building of the longhouse. She played a major part in seeing it reach fruition. When asked to share some words about the longhouse, Minnie stated, "It is something that many of us dreamed of for years. To our Native people, I hope it will be a home away from home. Once there is something like that in the university, maybe it will help the students."

Minnie received an honorary doctorate of laws from the University of British Columbia in May 1993. In speaking of the doctorate, she said, "It is wonderful to be recognized for something you believe in." Minnie has devoted many years to volunteer work with First Nations advisory boards, committees, and organizations.

Elder Vince Stogan was a member of the Musqueam Nation on whose traditional territory the university stands. His traditional name was Tsimilano. He was a healer who spent many winter hours taking part in longhouse traditions in Musqueam, the Lower Mainland, the Upper Fraser Valley, and southern Vancouver Island.

He was recognized by the University of British Columbia with an honorary doctorate of laws in 1995. He played a very important role in the building of the longhouse not only through the guidance and support he provided throughout the project but as a member of the Musqueam Nation. The longhouse is

Top: Simon Baker, Alvin Weget, Dominic Point, Vince Stogan, Minnie Croft, and Edna Stogan.

Bottom left: Dr Minnie Croft gives an address at a longhouse graduation ceremony.

Bottom right: Vince Stogan.

Photos: UBC ITServices, Telestudios

modelled after the shed-style Musqueam longhouse. Vince was for all of us, an excellent and patient teacher, instructing us in the protocol of the Musqueam as we marked each stage of the construction of the longhouse.

Vince's contributions to UBC were many, and even long after the longhouse was completed he continued to be an advisor, teacher, and mentor to the students and staff. He served on the First Nations House of Learning President's Advisory Committee and opened many UBC gatherings with a special prayer and welcoming words. His untimely death on 28 June 2000 leaves a large void in the life of the longhouse.

Elder Chief Simon Baker's Squamish name is Khot-La-Cha, meaning "Man with a kind heart." He has been aptly described by the Sechelt Nation as "an ambassador of his own culture and of the human spirit." At age ninety, he continues to promote First Nations cultures and to provide direction and guidance to all who seek his advice.

Simon received an honorary doctorate of laws from the University of British Columbia in 1993. He has given his time generously to help First Nations students through his involvement with the Native Indian Teacher Education Program, the First Nations House of Learning, and the building of the longhouse.

He played a special role in raising funds for the longhouse. As he was often asked to attend functions having to do with First Nations causes, he took advantage of these situations to raise money. At such a function in Whistler, BC, he told the audience about the longhouse project. When he got up to entertain, he said, "All of you sitting there, pick someone at your table. I want each of you to donate to the longhouse ... I'm going to entertain you now. If I get a lot of money, I'll entertain all night." From the audience of 200 that evening, he raised $1,400.

Elder Alfred Scow belongs to the Kwicksutaineuk tribe of the Kwakwaka'wakw Nation and comes from Alert Bay. He received his LL.B. from the University of British Columbia and was called to the bar in 1962. Alfred was the first Aboriginal lawyer in British Columbia.

Alfred has served on many boards and committees, including the UBC Alumni Association board, the UBC Senate, and with the First Nations House of Learning on the Longhouse Building Committee, two selection committees, and the Longhouse Management Council. In recognition of his devoted service, Alfred Scow received an honorary doctorate of law in 1994 and a Great Trekker Award in 1995 from the University of British Columbia. The award recognizes outstanding alumni and commemorates the 1922 student march and demonstration to persuade the provincial government to fund a new UBC campus.

He says about his work with First Nations at UBC, "I first became involved with the First Nations House of Learning at the sod turning ceremony in 1991. Recalling my own struggles, I was anxious to help establish a resource for First Nations students which would give them the recognition, support, and encouragement that was not available in my student days. It is indeed, a dream come true – Verna's dream – that will benefit present and future generations of students, the university, and Canadian society."

Joan Scow married Alfred Scow in 1964 and is an Elder herself. She received her master of social work degree from UBC in 1962. Joan played an important role in the building of the longhouse, giving generously of her time and expertise. She served on the Longhouse Building Committee.

Joan is very proud of the longhouse, which she describes as a place that will not only prepare our students to take their rightful place in society but that also establishes an Aboriginal presence on the campus. In speaking of her involvement with the Longhouse Building Committee, she said, "It was a great experience to see how culturally attuned the staff and students were and how tenacious they were about having their needs met by the longhouse that was being built. One such incident was a time when there was the fear that the

Top: Chief Simon Baker sings his deer dance song at a longhouse graduation ceremony.
Photo: The Media Group, Woodward Instructional Resources Centre, UBC

Bottom: Judge Alfred Scow and Joan Scow at the housepost raising ceremony. The Scows served on the Longhouse Building Committee.
Photo: Larry McFarland Architects

$5 million required would not be forthcoming. It was suggested by the university that the daycare be dropped from the plans. Our committee rejected the idea and refused to cut their cloth according to the finances available. Verna held on to the idea and went out and found $250,000. It is a great testimony to the vision that fired the whole project, a beautiful creation story."

Advocates

Dr David W. Strangway became president of the University of British Columbia in 1987. His interest in First Nations initiatives at UBC goes back to his arrival. In 1984, a report had been completed by an ad hoc committee struck by the former president, George Pedersen. The committee, co-chaired by Tom Berger and me, had been mandated to advise the president on how the university might better meet the needs of First Nations students and their communities. The main recommendation was that the university should establish an institute for the advancement of First Nations by offering a wide range of studies, relevant research, and support for students.

The Donner Canadian Foundation had indicated that they would consider providing the seed money for such an institute. Realizing the importance that the First Nations university community still placed on this recommendation three years later, Dr Strangway urged me to pursue the funding: "Well, why don't you go for it!" I did secure the funding, and the First Nations House of Learning began operation in the fall of 1987. Members were appointed to the President's Advisory Committee. One of the objectives decided upon was to build a physical facility – a longhouse – on the campus. During the World of Opportunity Campaign, Dr Strangway made the building of a longhouse a priority. In short, as head of the university, he demonstrated a commitment that led to the realization of our dream.

Dr Daniel R. Birch was Vice President Academic and Provost during the years the longhouse was being built. His interest in First Nations preceded his arrival at UBC in 1982. As Dean of Education at Simon Fraser University, he had initiated a teacher education program on the Mount Currie Reserve, near Pemberton, British Columbia. He came to UBC as Dean of Education. As dean, he was a great support to the Native Indian Teacher Education Program, and we accomplished a lot during that time. Later, as director of the First Nations House of Learning, I reported to him.

I appreciated Dan's understanding of the challenges that face First Nations people. When it came to building a longhouse on campus, he worked very hard to get the funding we needed to proceed with the plan.

We were able to count on his total support. He remarked, "The First Nations Longhouse is an important symbol representing the increasingly substantial presence of First Nations people in the programs of the university. It will be a meeting place for First Nations people and those of other cultures – a home away from home for First Nations students, where their heritage and cultures are not only reflected in the building but also represented in many activities."

Thomas R. Berger, QC, was born in 1933 in Victoria, British Columbia. He studied law at the University of British Columbia, graduating with a B.A. and an LL.B. in 1956. Berger practised law in Vancouver from 1957 to 1971. He was appointed to the Supreme Court of British Columbia in 1971 and served on the bench until September 1983. Berger has headed three royal commissions of inquiry, all of which affected Aboriginal people. He is the author of several books and the recipient of numerous awards for his outstanding work. He continues to be a strong advocate for Native rights.

Tom Berger co-chaired the 1984 ad hoc committee whose recommendations led to the creation of the First Nations House of Learning and subsequently, the First Nations Longhouse. He chaired the First Nations House of Learning Advisory Committee from 1987 to 1993.

Larry McFarland is the principal of Larry McFarland

Architects, based in Vancouver. He has a wide cross-section of experience in the planning and design of significant architectural projects since graduating with a bachelor's degree in architecture from the University of British Columbia in 1970.

His particular areas of expertise include programming, functional design studies, building systems development, design co-ordination, and project management. The First Nations Longhouse at UBC is one of Mr McFarland's most prominent commissions. He received the 1994 Governor General's Award for Architecture, the 1994 Canadian Wood Council Merit Award, and the 1995 Canadian Society of Landscape Architects' Regional Citation Award for the project.

Verna J. Kirkness was an associate professor and director of the First Nations House of Learning when the longhouse was being built. Verna's accomplishments during her time at the University of British Columbia (1981-93) are notable. In 1984, she played a key role in the development of Ts"kel Graduate Studies, a program in education for First Nations. In 1987, she became the founding director of the First Nations House of Learning, a unique concept designed to provide more opportunities and support for First Nations students. She spearheaded and co-ordinated the building of the $5 million longhouse, the first of its kind on a North American campus. Verna, who is Cree, has received many awards for her work, including the Order of Canada (1999), three honorary degrees, a National Aboriginal Achievement Award (1994), and Canadian Educator of the Year (1990).

William Bellman was born in Bowmanville, Ontario, and attended the University of Toronto. He joined CBC Ottawa in 1945. He moved to Vancouver in 1948, where he had a very successful career at CBC with the national radio program *A Man and His Music* and the national current affairs television show *Almanac*. In 1959, he founded CHQM, Vancouver's "good music" station. Within three years, the station was a top money maker in the Canadian radio market. William Bellman's personality was one of the key factors in its success. In 1976, he and others founded CKVU TV.

Mr Bellman donated $1 million to the construction of the First Nations Longhouse. Prior to the completion of the building, he spoke of his hopes for the longhouse: "The long-range benefits will be considerable as more and more First Nations people feel at home in the University and begin to get into higher education because I think that's the single most promising activity to get engaged in."

On 19 March 1995, the President's Office and the First Nations House of Learning hosted a donor appreciation luncheon and unveiled three copper plaques acknowledging the three major donors, their First Nations names, and the First Nations who gave them their names. William Bellman recalled a significant event that made him realize the importance of the longhouse: "On the night of the official opening, I was leaving the building to get the car from the parking lot next door. I passed a group of Native people, being sociable and talking to each other. As I passed, one person said in a soft but clear voice, "Thank you." Believe me, that impressed me more than anything else that's happened. The biggest ingredient I've noticed since the building has opened is the wonderful pride the local people here show in this building. There is a feeling of pride you can feel all through the building. This is probably the only building of its kind anywhere. I am proud to have been a part of it."

William Bellman passed away in 2000. Chief Simon Baker, who bestowed the name "X̱wi7x̱wa" on him, agreed that his son, David, would inherit his name. A naming ceremony was held for David Bellman in Sty-Wet-Tan on 15 August 2000.

Jack Bell is a Montrealer who came to the University of British Columbia in 1934 to finish his university degree. He was a member of the Kappa Theta Rho, the first Jewish fraternity at the university. He returned to

eastern Canada and, in 1941, joined the Air Sea Rescue Squadron. He came out west with the Air Force in 1944 and has remained in British Columbia ever since.

He made millions of dollars from peat moss and cranberry property on Lulu Island. Having done so well, he says, "I sold my peat moss business and my cranberry farm and I had more than enough to live on comfortably and so did my kids. So, with their co-operation, I developed guidelines for giving my money away."

The Vancouver General Hospital received $3 million from Bell and named their new facility on Oak Street the Jack Bell Research Centre. He also donated $1 million for geriatric research. Bell supported the Downtown Eastside Women's Centre when their dilapidated quarters needed replacement. The centre had asked the city for $20,000 to find decent accommodation. Jack Bell challenged the city to match his $10,000 gift. His tactics worked and the city met the challenge.

During the 19 March 1995 donor appreciation event, Jack Bell talked of the importance of the longhouse for students: "What we've done here is open a window of opportunity for Native students to come to a friendly, congenial atmosphere. They can use this longhouse and their education as a stepping stone to go forth into the world and help their people and the rest of the world."

Top: William and June Bellman receive a paddle and drum from Chief Simon and Emily Baker as Mr Bellman receives the name X̱wi7x̱wa.
Photo: David Neel

Bottom: Dave Joe Sr, of Musqueam, prepares Jack Bell for his naming ceremony. Mr Bell was given a Salish blanket woven by Margaret Louis of Musqueam.
Photo: Pat Higinbotham — Studio 54

James Wallace receives the Gitxsan name Wii Ax.

Photo: David Neel

During the 1960s and 1970s, James Wallace owned and operated Wallace Neon Company, a neon sign and billboard enterprise. He was also involved in real estate investments. He is owner and president of San Rafael Racing Stables and has also established the James B. Wallace Foundation.

At the 19 March 1995 donor appreciation ceremony, Mr Wallace was presented with a gold carved pendant from Chief Alvin Weget, Gitxsan Nation. Chief Weget sang a traditional song and told the story of the Wii Ax fern crest. Afterwards, James Wallace said, "I am deeply honoured ... [It] brings tears to my eyes. The Native people played a big part in my life. My grandfather was a seal hunter. He had a Native wife. So, as the wheel goes around, the wheel comes around."

Living the Dream

JO-ANN ARCHIBALD

A WEEK IN THE LIFE OF THE LONGHOUSE

Early Monday morning I walk along the pathway from the parkade to the northern entrance of the longhouse and approach the Sacred Circle structure. The sunlight filters through its copper roof opening, giving a radiant light. As I sit on the rocks under this structure, I admire the circular ceiling and feel the calmness of the warm morning air. The joyful sound of the waterfall beside the X̱wi7x̱wa Library echoes to this place. The Sacred Circle is used for ceremony, prayer, and reflection. The trees, grass, and plants have their own special beauty. A few years ago, we decided to let this area grow naturally and asked the university gardeners not to cut the grass. In this natural learning environment, our Elders teach the students about plant knowledge. I am thankful for this peaceful moment in our special spiritual sanctuary.

The smell of cedar greets me when I open the entrance door. I look at the board in the reception area that lists the events booked for this week. Sty-Wet-Tan is heavily scheduled. Michael, the Ts''kel Graduate Studies director, is conducting one of his education classes in the hall. Verena, our co-ordinator of Student Services, is hosting an adult education class from Merritt. They are learning about the various programs offered at UBC and the type of student services we provide. Elders from the Port Hardy area will be here on Wednesday. I know that the students will enjoy visiting them. Gordon, the First Nations Forestry co-ordinator, is hosting a cultural awareness session for his faculty. The little children from the S-Takya childcare centre will be in the hall twice during the week to play games for their physical fitness activity. The sound of children having fun provides enjoyment to the staff. June, the director of First Nations Legal Studies, is hosting an orientation for the twenty new first-year students, who come from across Canada. The Institute for Aboriginal Health is holding its community council meeting here on Thursday. On Thursday evening, a potluck dinner will be sponsored by the First Nations Student Association. I'm looking forward to the great feast that will be shared. On Friday night, Nicola, one of the students in the Native Indian Teacher Education Program, is organizing the first Aboriginal Coffee House of the year. Students and anyone from the community can get up on stage and read their work, sing, and tell stories. I am amazed at the

Student Services

ACADEMIC SUPPORT

- academic planning through staff in First Nations programs (e.g., NITEP, First Nations Legal Studies, First Nations Health Carers, Ts"kel Graduate Studies)
- academic planning through First Nations Advisors/Coordinators in faculties (Arts, Forestry)
- tutoring in course work (limited funding available)
- peer tutoring
- feedback on papers
- seminars for graduate students
- participation on graduate student committees
- computer lab
- X̱wi7x̱wa Library
- guest speakers
- workshops: Longhouse Student Leadership Program

FINANCIAL SUPPORT

- scholarships and bursaries
- financial assistance information
- liaison with UBC Awards and Financial Aid
- referrals to other services both on- and off-campus
- employment opportunities

PERSONAL SUPPORT

- First Nations counsellors
- all staff provide some support to the best of their ability
- student organizations: First Nations Student Association, First Nations Law Student Association, Association of Aboriginal Graduate Students, Students for Aboriginal Health

- Elders-in-Residence Program
- Peer Support Network
- talking circles
- sweat lodge
- special interest activities (e.g., Tai Chi, art therapy)
- collaborations with and referrals to on-campus counselling services (e.g., Women Students' Office, Student Counselling and Resources Centre, Pacific Spirit Family and Community Services)
- referrals to other services, both on- and off-campus
- orientations: "Student Services at UBC," "Meet the Vancouver Aboriginal Community"
- assured housing for single students (50 units)
- childcare centre
- social activities (potlucks, Native Awareness Days, dinners, Christmas party, graduation celebrations, etc.)

CAREER SUPPORT

- networking with organizations, corporations, and government
- career fairs
- job postings
- role models
- employment opportunities

OTHER

- access to all UBC support services

talent. By day they are students and by night, at the coffee house, they are skilled musicians and writers.

The boardroom is also heavily booked, with various program meetings and a couple of evening classes. The NITEP co-ordinators from the Chilliwack, Duncan, and Kamloops field centres will be here for a couple of days of program planning. I must remember to attend the UBC Student Services and Longhouse Programs meeting. We meet once a month to discuss matters such as financial aid, recruitment, admissions, and the various services and resources we provide. Madeleine, our associate director, and Stacey, from the Registrar's Office, will update us on the enrolment results of the Aboriginal admissions policy. The X̱wi7x̱wa seminar room is used for a number of First Nations studies classes in education, health, and science. It looks as though this will be another busy week in the longhouse.

I listen for Alannah's gentle invitation to the staff in the Wii Ax administration area to join the Monday morning smudging ceremony. As she walks to the Elders' Room, she invites visitors and students to join us. Alannah is our counsellor, and this is one of her many responsibilities. I look forward to our Monday and Friday morning smudges. We form a circle. We burn a very small amount of plant medicines and let the smoke symbolically cleanse our space and our-

selves. A prayer is said and then each participant shares a few words. We close with a prayer and a song. I leave feeling connected to the Creator, to the people in the circle, and to the larger family of the longhouse.

The week quickly begins. I greet Kisha, one of our student longhouse hosts. She assists visitors and guests with their enquiries when they come to the reception desk. She is friendly and very helpful to new students who are anxious about finding their classrooms. Soon the students' laughter and talk fill the air. The staff program offices buzz with ringing phones and students coming in to share good news about assignments and personal issues and to discuss program matters. As I enter our boardroom for the longhouse staff meeting, I purposely sit facing the magnificent birch tree on the east side of the building, which stands among many different trees from all over the world and some native berry plants. This view of nature adds a dimension of tranquillity to my hectic pace.

At lunch hour, there is a lot of laughter, teasing, and serious discussion in the lounge. Caleb, one of the students, is encouraging people to sign up for intramural sports. He has volunteers for the longhouse hockey, basketball, and volleyball teams. Kirsten wants to have a longboat team for this year's races. Some students work on their assignments at the tables, seemingly

Top: Students Sharon Thorne and Lana Wright in the student and staff lounge.

Bottom: Te Tuhi Robust, Maori visiting scholar, relaxes in the student and staff lounge.

Photos: Angie Oleman

oblivious to the noise around them. Louie is sleeping on one of the couches. He must have stayed up until the wee hours of the morning working on a paper. I notice that the bulletin boards have been redesigned to look attractive and are neatly organized by topics such as employment, buy/sell/rent, counselling information, conferences and workshops, student associations, and program information. Students continue to come to their home away from home throughout the day to rest between classes, to work on assignments, or to visit one another.

The lounge is next to the computer lab, which is often their next stop. The lab is open twenty-four hours a day, seven days a week. Antoinetta, our computer lab co-ordinator, posts a notice for part-time student assistants to help her teach students how to use the various computer programs, to assist lab users with technical problems, and to maintain the computers.

I notice that Pat, our building manager, is also advertising for part-time student longhouse hosts to help with program and rental activities in Sty-Wet-Tan and to assist visitors who come to the reception area. I hear a group making arrangements to meet in the lounge early this evening for a tutoring session.

I remember that I must get some material from X̱wi7x̱wa Library in order to prepare for a series of lectures that I will be giving soon about the oral tradition and First Nations language programs. I have been invited to be a visiting scholar at a language and research centre at the University of Paris. Linda, our X̱wi7x̱wa library assistant, shows me all that is available about First Nations languages. She shows me curriculum materials, research papers, books, CDs, videos, journal articles, and a Web page with helpful links to other Web sites. Ann, the X̱wi7x̱wa librarian, teaches the student assistants basic library processing skills and more advanced information technology skills for developing Web reference pages. All the staff are known for their friendly, helpful, and knowledgeable ways.

X̱wi7x̱wa is a very useful resource to UBC students, faculty, First Nations communities, and the general public. It is living up to its Squamish name, which means "echo." The name recalls the way in which the echo can be used to help people find their way, signifying that the reciprocal, back and forth action of lending and returning material is beneficial. The library collection originates from the Indian Education Resource Centre, which was established in 1970 by the BC Native Indian Teachers' Association. In the early 1980s, the collection was given to the Native Indian Teacher Education Program (NITEP). Grants from the H.R. McMillan Foundation and Joseph S. Stauffer Foundation greatly enhanced the collection. NITEP donated the library collection to the First Nations House of Learning at the opening of the new facilities in 1993. The collection focuses on First Nations content. Gene Joseph, Wet'suwet'en Nation, the first graduate of Aboriginal ancestry in the Master of Library Science program at UBC, was X̱wi7x̱wa's first librarian. Gene was responsible for organizing the collection and for X̱wi7x̱wa's initial development.

X̱wi7x̱wa is currently open Monday to Friday, from 9:00 a.m. to 5:00 p.m., with two full-time staff, a librarian, and library assistant, and five to ten part-time student assistants. A March 2000 user survey brought many comments about the value of the library: "Just like going home. Staff is very approachable, knowledgeable and friendly. They can answer every question and even go out of their way to help"; "I love doing my homework in the library because it is so peaceful and I feel welcome. It is very cozy"; "Really good resource, this library. The staff is easily the friendliest, most helpful, and genuinely concerned with meeting your needs. I just wish I could pronounce X̱wi7x̱wa!"

I can't believe that Friday is already here. I relish the opportunity to participate in the smudging ceremony. It's been a full week of planning meetings with the various faculties, writing funding proposals and reports,

Top left: Angie Oleman, secretary for First Nations House of Learning, holds a drum that she has made.
Photo: Tania Wahbe

Top right: N'kixw'stn James, an instructor in the Longhouse Elders-in-Residence program, sits in the Elders' Room.
Photo: Angie Oleman

Bottom: Student Darrel Ryan concentrates during a cedar-bark weaving workshop.
Photo: Angie Oleman

assisting graduate students with their theses and dissertations, attending problem-solving sessions with the program staff about really tough issues that students are experiencing, and being involved with Vancouver area Aboriginal organizations on education and health matters. The smudge will help me to centre my thoughts and determine priorities for next week.

In the afternoon, our Elders-in-Residence, N'kixw'stn and John, come into the longhouse and walk through the staff area and then to the lounge to greet staff and students. Their smiles and caring manner have a positive effect. They each have a group of participants who meet them every Friday afternoon. The women students sit with N'kixw'stn in the Elders' Room. They conduct a talking circle, with each person given an opportunity to say whatever they need, and then they continue talking while sewing moccasins. John sits with the men students in the Living Cultures Room, which is beside the Elders' Room. They also engage in a talking circle and then work on their drum-making project. We've found that talking circles and traditional craft activities are very healing emotional activities. It's been great to have N'kixw'stn and John as our Elders for the past three years. They are a wife-and-husband team. They have mentored a number of our staff and have helped many students.

Clockwise, from upper left:

Verena Wilhelmson, co-ordinator of Student Services for the First Nations House of Learning, works on her project during a starblanket workshop.

Mary Jane Joe, NITEP co-ordinator, begins to weave a cedar-bark basket.

Shirley Bear, an Elder instructor, teaches about plants and herbs in the longhouse kitchen.

A sweat dress workshop teaches students how to make traditional garments.

Photos: Angie Oleman

Top: 1999 UBC Summer Session class taught by Dr Carolyn Kenny of Simon Fraser University. The class is standing in the area beside the waterfall.
Photo: Angie Oleman

Bottom: Students attend weekly drumming sessions in Sty-Wet-Tan.
Photo: Angie Oleman

Later in the afternoon, some community volunteers and students come into Sty-Wet-Tan with their hand drums and also set up the large NITEP powwow drum. The participants teach each other different kinds of drumming and songs. The sounds of the drumming and singing are food for my soul. I feel blessed to have a place, a longhouse, where we can practise ceremony, live our culture, be a family, develop academic programming, and learn from one another.

When I return to my office later in the day, I think about the times when our dear Elder, Vince Stogan, would drop by to visit. I treasure those memories because he recently passed to the Spirit World. Many times during the year, he would sit with me and have a cup of coffee and tell me about the communities he was asked to help and the ceremonies he conducted. He always asked how things were going, in his very caring way. Over the years, he gave encouragement and advice; he taught traditions and practices about respect for cultural knowledge, for spiritual matters, and for people; and he demonstrated gentle leadership. At UBC, he opened gatherings for many different groups, setting an atmosphere of respect and caring. He would often start with the greeting "My dear ones." Vince told us that he could never say no when asked to share his knowledge and ways with others.

Guests attend a conference
dinner in Sty-Wet-Tan.
Photo: Angie Oleman

I also think of other Elders such as Minnie Croft, Simon Baker, Alfred Scow, Joan Scow, Ellen White, Bob George, Bev Julian, and Ken Harris, who sit with us on UBC advisory councils and committees and who are Elders-in-Residence for various programs. Again, I feel blessed to have the privilege of learning from people who have such wisdom.

When I leave the building, I notice the student hosts helping Pat to get ready for a health conference that will take place in Sty-Wet-Tan this weekend. It's been another fulfilling week at the First Nations Longhouse.

THE TEACHINGS THAT GUIDE US

I think of the First Nations Longhouse as being truly a house of learning. Sty-Wet-Tan, with its carved house-posts, roof beams, and doors is like a curriculum that contains cultural knowledge and values. We often refer to this curriculum as "teachings." These teachings guide the ways in which longhouse staff work with others. The Sty-Wet-Tan houseposts, carved by First Nations artists from British Columbia, remind me of the good teachings that come from the Ancestors, Mother Earth, and Sky Father. These houseposts, like First Nations stories, engage me in a process of think-ing, feeling, and being. When I introduce the long-

house to guests invited to our gatherings, I say that I will take them on a "talking tour" of Sty-Wet-Tan. I and other staff use cultural teachings and stories of the houseposts, carved doors, and roof beams to exem-plify the purpose and initiatives of the First Nations House of Learning. The artists' carved figures take on special meaning as we live and interact with them.

Lyle Wilson's housepost speaks to me about the importance of extending and maintaining family rela-tionships. The Eagle and Beaver represent his Haisla family clan crests. Within the longhouse we nurture the extended family. Students may feel lonely and iso-lated at a huge learning institution like UBC, which has a student population of over 35,000. There is usu-ally someone to talk to, laugh with, or just sit with at the longhouse. Even though many Aboriginal cultures are represented in the student body, we have common teachings of respect, caring, and sharing. Many gradu-ates and former staff and faculty maintain family links with the longhouse even after they leave UBC.

Lyle also carved a ceremonial door with an Eagle design, which is used only for very special occasions. For many First Nations, the Eagle symbolizes signifi-cant achievement. It may seem like a plain door, but the design is meaningful in its simplicity. In late May of each year, we host a longhouse graduation

Students' Voices

I could go and sit alone in the great hall, Sty-Wet-Tan, and collect myself and my thoughts. The great hall is a place where I went to surround myself with peace and quiet and when I felt re-energized, I was able to carry on with my studies. The longhouse is a place where I could go and visit with family and friends and it is a place where I could always find a smiling face.

DEBORAH L. WILSON, NITEP GRADUATE, MAY 2000

A few years back, I attended a graduation ceremony at the longhouse. I didn't know anybody graduating at the time. I only wanted to go watch. As the graduates were being recognized, family and friends clapped and cheered them on. I became quite emotional at all this celebration. Later, I was trying to understand what brought about all those feelings I had that day. I came to understand that, despite being so far away from my family and community, I still belonged to a larger community of People, the community of the longhouse.

JAN HARE, DOCTORAL STUDENT IN EDUCATION

celebration for the First Nations students. There is loud applause when graduates walk through the ceremonial door to be introduced. Families and friends fill Sty-Wet-Tan and offer their support and love once more. It fills me with joy to witness the achievement of these future teachers, lawyers, health care professionals, foresters, entrepreneurs, scientists, and well-educated citizens. They have completed one cycle of learning and sharing. I know that many of these graduates will return the gift of learning, caring, and support to the next generation that attends postsecondary education.

Whenever I introduce Stan Bevan and Ken McNeil's housepost to a group, I talk about the importance of maintaining a constant Aboriginal cultural identity throughout all the transformative life experiences we encounter. When I look at the housepost it seems to me as if a human form changes into a Raven, then back to human form. When students come to the university to learn new knowledge and skills, they experience many changes. Many come from small communities, they may leave family and friends, their children start new schools, and they learn to be university students. In our stories, the Raven's experiences remind us to stay connected to the good teachings that come from our communities, the land, and the Ancestors. Raven often gets into trouble when he forgets to stay connected.

Clockwise, from upper left:

Art Azak stands outside the ceremonial door at graduation.

Two views of guests at a longhouse graduation ceremony.

Kirsten Baker and Carla George sing a traditional song during a longhouse graduation ceremony.

Photos: The Media Group, Woodward Instructional Resources Centre, UBC

Top: 1998 graduates.

Bottom: Michael Yellow Bird, former faculty member of the UBC School of Social Work, performs a traditional dance.
Photo: The Media Group, Woodward Instructional Resources Centre, UBC

These positive teachings will help sustain us in troubling times. One of our Elders, Ellen White, says that we need to learn and honour the "core" of who we are as Aboriginal people. I have learned that a strong cultural identity, a cultural core, is invaluable for coping with educational change. The Raven in his many transformations also symbolizes strength of knowledge.

Our First Nations House of Learning logo, designed by Tsimshian artist Glen Wood, depicts the strength of Raven to make positive institutional change at UBC. Glen attended the Gitanmax School of Northwest Coast Art at K'san in Hazelton, BC. He also works in silver, gold, and ivory, using engraving, chasing, repoussé, and casting techniques. He has worked with other artists such as Dempsey Bob, Gerry Marks, Norman Tait, Art Thompson, Robert Davidson, and Reggie Davidson on large poles commissioned by the City of Prince Rupert, the Maclean Hunter Building in Toronto, the National Museum of Ethnology in Osaka, Japan, the UBC Museum of Anthropology, and the UBC Psychology Building. Glen's art is published in several books, including *Indian Artists at Work,* by Ulli Steltzer, and *Totem Poles,* by Hilary Stewart. His design for the First Nations House of Learning logo shows a mirrored image of Raven on a house-shaped structure that represents the university. The human face under the house structure

symbolizes the students. The First Nations House of Learning uses the transformative function attributed to Raven to make positive institutional change at UBC. I believe that the mission statement of the First Nations House of Learning is more relevant than ever:

The mandate of the First Nations House of Learning is to make the University's vast resources more accessible to First Peoples, and to improve the University's ability to meet the needs of First Nations. To this end, the House of Learning seeks direction from First Nations communities in determining priorities and approaches taken. We are dedicated to quality preparation in all fields of postsecondary study. We believe that quality education is determined by its relevance to the philosophy and values of First Nations and guided through the "voices of our ancestors."

The House of Learning has made institutional change through a university-wide Aboriginal admissions policy, by assisting faculties with the development and implementation of relevant academic programs, by increasing First Nations staff and faculty positions, and by ensuring community input and direction. When the First Nations House of Learning began in 1987, ten community consultations were held across the province. Students, parents, community leaders, and workers identified five fields of study that should be given priority: education, health, natural resource sciences, business, and First Nations

languages. The consultations were offered in workshop format. Participants were asked to identify professionals already working in their communities and to recommend the professional fields that the community needed but lacked. Often they created an ideal vision of their community and were then able to prioritize their educational needs. The House of Learning works with the faculties of arts, education, law, health sciences, graduate studies, forestry, applied science, science, agricultural sciences, and commerce and business administration to develop and support educational programs and courses.

Bradley Hunt's carved doors, which separate Sty-Wet-Tan from the foyer, remind me of the continuing need to build individual and community capacity through education. A split image of the salmon jumping contains human figures within the fish and at the base of the design. The salmon and the people are in a symbiotic relationship. The salmon was and is an essential resource for the First Nations of British Columbia. I believe that education is like our salmon, an essential resource. We must ensure that postsecondary education is used to build capacity for strong communities.

When I look at the salmon carving, I also think about an innovative program we are initiating with the Faculty of Commerce and Business Administration, called the Chinook Program. It includes both high school and

UBC Aboriginal Admissions Policy

CANADIAN ABORIGINAL STUDENTS

The University of British Columbia is dedicated to making the University's vast resources more accessible to Aboriginal People, and to improving the University's ability to meet their educational needs. The University recognizes that Aboriginal students can make valuable contributions to its learning environment and therefore invites inquiries and applications from Aboriginal candidates to its many and diverse fields of study. Those who do not meet the current academic standing set by the individual faculties and schools, but who meet the university-wide academic minimum of 67% for first year programs, will be considered on an individual basis by the applicable faculty or school and a representative of the First Nations House of Learning. Educational history, cultural knowledge, work experience, educational goals, and achievements that indicate an ability to succeed at university will be considered.

Each applicant must submit two letters of reference from persons specifically able to assess the applicant's potential for academic success. One reference letter should be from a recognized Aboriginal organization or community leader. Applicants must also submit a personal letter outlining their academic objectives.

For the purpose of application and admission to the University of British Columbia, and in accordance with the *Constitution Act of 1982, Part II, Section 35 (2)*, an Aboriginal applicant is an Indian, Inuit, or Métis person of Canada.

undergraduate education components. Chinook was the first trade language used by First Nations and European traders in British Columbia. The logo of the Chinook Program also has a salmon design, signifying the importance of salmon for commerce.

The high school component of the program is called 1st N-STEP (First Nations Student Entrepreneurship Program). It features case studies of successful Aboriginal entrepreneurs and businesses. Senior high school students will learn from these case studies and develop business plans for innovative business endeavours. They will enter a team competition and present their plans at the First Nations Longhouse each spring and meet some of the Aboriginal business people and university students.

The undergraduate education component will form alliances between the university and community colleges and First Nations postsecondary institutions. This component will build on the successful principles of the Native Indian Teacher Education Program, in which students complete the first two years of study at regional centres such as community colleges and then transfer to the university campus to complete their senior degree studies. First Nations courses, internships, and student support will be important components for success. I look forward to moving ahead with this initiative because First Nations are extremely under-represented in the Commerce faculty.

The Chinook Program also borrows components from the successful Synala Honours Program. Synala is a Kwak'wala term that means "the circle is complete." For five to six weeks, each summer from 1992 to 1999, the First Nations House of Learning and First Nations Health Careers/Institute for Aboriginal Health offered a university orientation program to twenty to thirty First Nations students who had completed Grade 11. About 217 students completed the program. The students lived in the university student residence, attended courses in English, math, First Nations studies, ethnobotany, and career exploration/college knowledge. The program emphasized a holistic approach with cultural and traditional teachings of the Elders, academic skill preparation, recreation, and planning for postsecondary education. Many of our students and alumni work as staff of the program, providing instruction, mentoring, and guidance.

During July and August, our longhouse was filled with youth, energy, hope, and excitement about the future. Students often got homesick when the program started, but by the end of their rigorous program, they often did not want to go home. They had formed strong bonds of friendship with classmates and the

Synala high school youth program participants at their graduation.
Photo: UBC ITServices, Telestudios

Pow-wow fancy dancer.
Photo: Alan Katowitz

staff. Graduation day was one of the highlights for me. I vividly remember their smiles of happiness and pride as they posed for their grad group photo. Sty-Wet-Tan was filled with families and friends witnessing the Synala students' accomplishments. Over the years, a number of the Synala students have enrolled at UBC, and they comment that the program gave them the courage and preparation to apply. My hope for the Chinook Program is to enable Aboriginal high school youth to learn about business career possibilities, have a welcoming introduction to UBC, and feel positive about completing high school and continuing to post-secondary education.

Returning to the "talking tour," I note that Walter and his son, Rod Harris, gave us a housepost that represents them: a father and son learning and working together. When I look at this housepost with the wolf holding its pup, I am reminded that the work of the First Nations House of Learning must benefit the younger and future generations. We take on this important responsibility to do our work with care and love for those who come after us. The three human figures that stand on the wolf's shoulders represent the students who come to learn at UBC. They are held up by the love, support, and teachings that come from their families and communities.

I often think that the human figures can also represent the people who work at UBC. They stand side by side to symbolize working together for the benefit of First Nations. The figure in the middle is speaking while the outside two figures listen. We are thus reminded to listen much more than we speak. The Elders also teach us to listen with our three ears: two on the sides of our head and the one in our heart. We learn to bring the heart and mind, the three ears, together.

We come to Susan Point's post, which is a representation of Raven in two different forms. One Raven stands proudly, watching like an owl. His wing feathers, held closely to his body, remind me of a Coast Salish blanket. He stands on a circular spindle whorl, which shows another Raven and a human face. As women spun the wool of the mountain goat to make blankets, the wool was wound onto a long stick that had a circular, carved spindle whorl at one end. Raven is honouring the traditional work of women.

I believe that the circular shape of the spindle whorl symbolizes a holistic approach to the work of the First Nations House of Learning. The intellectual, spiritual, emotional, and physical realms must all be nourished for a person to receive quality education. Students come to UBC to pursue all fields of knowledge. In the intellectual realm, the House of Learning assists with

Top left: Guests at the annual Longhouse Volunteer Appreciation Luncheon participate in a traditional dance.

Top right: Mary Jane Joe and Jo-ann Archibald serving baked bannock from the kitchen adjacent to Sty-Wet-Tan.

Bottom: Students learn to play a traditional guessing game called slahal.

Photos: Angie Oleman

Following page, photo: Steven Evans

the development of new First Nations courses, such as "The Role of Aboriginal Women in Canada" with the Women's Studies Programme in the Faculty of Arts and "First Nations Health" with the Institute for Aboriginal Health. In the spiritual realm, we provide individual and group opportunities and places for prayer and ceremonies. Our student services team helps students deal with emotional issues. Our counselling approaches include both traditional activities and conventional techniques. In the physical realm, food is often available for sharing in the longhouse. I often tell potential students that they will not "go hungry" if they come to the longhouse. The physical realm also includes sports and traditional dancing. One year Lee, one of our students, taught powwow dancing. It was a fun way to fitness. As well, students such as Lee assume many different leadership roles through teaching others and leading activities.

Our Elders also teach us that everyone is welcome in the circle. Non-Aboriginal people are invited to share our space and to listen and learn with others. The Musqueam Elders have also given us the responsibility to be good hosts to those who visit us. We honour first the cultural protocols of the Musqueam and Coast Salish peoples, as we are in their traditional territory.

When I look at the ends of the magnificent roof beams of the longhouse, carved by Don Yeomans, which show a Killer Whale and a Sea Lion, I can still picture them being carefully placed on the houseposts during the unveiling ceremony in 1992. Such beauty and strength was brought together with exceptional skill, precision, and dedication. As I walk along the boardwalk toward the building's eastern entrance and look up to the Killer Whale and Sea Lion figures, their prominence makes me feel that the teachings of the Ancestors are strong and will continue forever.

Remembering

I'm nearing the end of my tenure as the director of the First Nations House of Learning. I followed in Verna's footsteps and began shortly after the longhouse opened. I remember the move into the building in 1993. Excitement filled the building. The smell of cedar permeated the air. Rarely have I experienced a "dream come true." I was used to the offices in the old army huts behind the Scarfe (Education) building, which were cramped but intimate quarters. The longhouse felt huge, with lots of open space. The massive houseposts and roof beams made me feel small. But what a beautiful house of learning. It wasn't long before this magnificent longhouse became my second home.

For eight years, I have had a beautiful home in which to work. The longhouse stands as a significant and strong physical presence on the university campus. It is rooted in the traditional knowledge of Aboriginal peoples, and its foundation contains the values that help us to be good human beings to each other and to elements of nature.

As I walk through the longhouse late on a quiet afternoon, I think of many memorable moments in Sty-Wet-Tan: the wonderful speeches, songs, dances, and heartfelt discussions. Indigenous guests have shared common issues and their culture. Couples have been married here. International music and story-telling festivals have been held here. Taking one last walk through the natural surroundings of the S-Takya playground, I wonder how many of the children who have attended our daycare centre will follow in their parents' footsteps and come to UBC when they graduate from high school.

In 1993, after the longhouse was completed, I had worked on starting up the daycare, planning programs, securing the childcare centre licence, and ensuring that the playground was completed. A new Longhouse Childcare Centre Planning Committee was established with representation from UBC Aboriginal students

Top and bottom: Our beautiful daycare is for the children of today's students, the students of tomorrow.

Photos: George Vaitkunas

with young children, staff, and others with expertise in early childhood education. From January 1994 to March 1995, the committee held planning sessions to discuss the proposed childcare centre's philosophy, equipping the physical facility, designing the playground, developing a First Nations program, and staffing. We were fortunate to have a prominent early childhood education visiting Maori scholar, Carol Garden, assist us. Carol volunteered her services as part-time co-ordinator for the centre for one year.

The initial childcare centre proposal called for a family grouping approach, in which infants, toddlers, and preschool children would be in the same physical facility. This type of childcare resonated with the extended family concept that is central to Aboriginal cultures. A request for licence variance was made to the Ministry of Health. We were fortunate to obtain this licence because there are very few in the province of British Columbia. Normally, licensed childcare centres are required to have completely separate physical facilities for children over and under three years of age.

As well as helping to fund the construction of the playground, the Vancouver Foundation also provided funding for the development of First Nations curriculum and activities. An annual First Nations theme calendar based on seasonal activities was developed and

Outdoor playground area of the
S-Takya childcare centre.
Photo: Bentley Wong

continues to be used. For the cultural program, parents, longhouse staff, and Elders volunteer to share cultural songs, dances, and stories. Many of the learning materials have First Nations content or highlight nature. On 10 March 1997, the children and staff hosted a potlatch and ceremony, to witness Elder Dominic Point of the Musqueam Nation officially name our centre S-Takya, which in his Hun'q'umin'um language means "wolf." He chose this name from a Musqueam story about wolves because the story and the wolf remind us about the importance of a family that cares for and supports one another.

Our S-Takya childcare centre is 161 square metres and is licensed for a total of sixteen children of from six months to five years. Infants, toddlers, and preschoolers share the physical facilities but four different rooms are used for various purposes. One small room has infant cribs and change tables. Another is a quiet room for looking at and reading books. Two other rooms serve purposes such as listening to music, gross motor activities, art projects, engaging in age-appropriate learning theme units, naps, and eating snacks and lunch. Throughout the day, the children are together for many of the activities, though the preschoolers spend some time each day apart from the others in order to address their learning needs.

A senior supervisor, two early childhood educators, one half-time assistant, and student assistants staff the centre. It is open from Monday to Friday, from 8:00 a.m. to 5:00 p.m. One parent's comment sums up the benefits of family grouping childcare:

Being from a large family myself (youngest of eight), the mixed age grouping of this daycare seems very natural, more natural than the segregated groupings of other daycares. As more and more of us have smaller families, it is essential for the healthy socialization of our children to find "substitutes" for the extended family. Daycare can help to fill that void, and having mixed ages in the daycare allows our kids to develop healthy social behaviours with other children, both younger and older than themselves.

Through the physical surroundings, the choice of playthings, arts and crafts, and through the staff and volunteers, [my child] is exposed to First Nations traditions in a very positive way.

As I finish my last look at the longhouse, I take time to sit in the Elders' Room and sense that the Elders are watching and smiling with joy because their teachings continue. I am especially thankful to the Elders whose wisdom, strength, and endurance helped in the realization of this dream: Simon Baker for his special way of raising money and making people feel at ease, Vince and Edna Stogan for conducting the important ceremonies, Minnie Croft for her ardent encouragement and support, and Alfred and Joan Scow for their respectful guidance.

I hear the echo of the students' voices throughout the longhouse. Their voices speak about the quality education that brings together different forms of knowledge to benefit Aboriginal people and their communities. They speak about their joys, sorrows, challenges, and achievements at UBC and how their longhouse family helped them. It has been a privilege to live the dream begun by many others keenly interested in making the university more accessible and responsive to First Nations. It has been a privilege to work with the dedicated, skilled, and caring staff who have made the longhouse a home away from home for students and guests. As I turn out the lights and leave, I know that I will return often to be a part of the First Nations Longhouse family traditions.

HANDS BACK, HANDS FORWARD

As we come to the conclusion of sharing our dream, Verna and I hope that the teachings that were given to us can be useful to you some day. We hope that our experiences will help anyone planning to build a longhouse or a house of learning that reflects Aboriginal values and traditional Aboriginal architecture. We have shared what we learned and what others taught us about creating and living in a "dream" place that honours Aboriginal cultures and peoples. We urge you to dream and to live your dreams to the fullest. As we close this book, we smile as we remember and practise the teaching of Vince Stogan, Tsimilano, about "hands back, hand forward."

We ask you to form a circle and join hands in prayer. As we join hands, we hold the left palm upward to reach back and receive the teachings of the Ancestors. We learn these teachings and let them become a part of us. When we hold the right palm downward, we pass these teachings to the younger generation. In this way, the teachings of the Ancestors continue, and the circle of human understanding and caring grows stronger.

All My Relations, Ho!

Initial Members of the First Nations House of Learning Advisory Committee

Donors

Dr Owen Anderson, Regional Director General, Indian and Northern Affairs, BC Region

Gordon Antoine, Nlaka'pamux, Nicola Valley Indian Administration

Jo-ann Archibald, Sto:lo, NITEP Supervisor

Thomas R. Berger, Chair, lawyer

Christie Brown, Manager, Provincial Ministry of Advanced Education and Job Training

Kerry Charnley, secretary, First Nations Health Care Professions Program

Minnie Croft, Haida Elder

Ethel B. Gardner, Sto:lo, Assistant Director, First Nations House of Learning

Collette Good, Coast Salish, NITEP student representative

Mary Jane Jim, Tlingit/Southern Tutchone Yukon community representative

Dean Robert Kennedy, Forestry, UBC

Verna Kirkness, Cree, Director, First Nations House of Learning

Bert McKay, Nisga'a, Co-chair, Native Indian Education Advisory Committee

Allan Mason, Heiltsuk, Coordinator, First Nations Health Care Professions Program

Kathryn Morven, Nisga'a, secretary, First Nations House of Learning

Philip Paul, Chairman and Administrator, Saanich Indian School Board

Ron Peigan, Sioux/Cree, Native Law Program, student representative

Associate Dean N. Robin Riley, Faculty of Science, Student Services

Joan Ryan, Gitxsan, Co-chair, Native Indian Education Advisory Committee

Sam Stevens, Algonquin, Director, Native Law Program

Vince Stogan, Musqueam Elder

Oscar Swanson, Nisga'a, Native Indian Student Union representative

Minnie Croft always greeted each donation with the words, "It doesn't matter if it is a million dollars or one dollar, thanks a million!" To date, many generous hearts have contributed to the construction of this home for First Nations learners. These benefactors include Jack Bell, who contributed $1 million, William E. and June Bellman, who also contributed $1 million, and James and Ilse Wallace, who provided an additional $500,000. The Province of British Columbia matched all donations up to $2.3 million through the University of British Columbia's World of Opportunity Campaign. The Ministry of Advanced Education donated a further $211,000 toward the construction of the daycare.

Shirley Adams
Jackie Agostinis
James H. Andrew
Anglican Church of Canada, General Synod
Anspayaxw School Society
Archdiocese of Vancouver
Lorna Azak
Dr Jean C. Barman

Jack T. Bell, CM, OBC, LLD
William E. and June Bellman
Hon. Thomas R. Berger, OC, QC
Beda Louise Blain
Wendy L. Bolton
Maria Bouwman
E. Louise Brooks
Marjorie J. Brown
Rennie Bert Brown
Margaret Brunette
Katherine H. Capes
Carlson Wagonlit Travel
Anne and Angus Carmichael
Carrier Sekani Tribal Council
Elizabeth D. Carter
Norman N. Carter
Melton C.M. Charters
Coldwater Indian Band
Cook's Ferry Indian Band
Dr Charlotte Coombs
Cowichan Indian Band
James William Coyne
Marilyn L. Cram
Charlotte Elva Dill
Dr Murray Elliott
Dr William S.B. Forman
Ethel Berdie Gardner
William Gaspard
Doug Gill
Gitksan Wet'suwet'en Local Services Society
Genevieve M. Gleason
Vincent V. Gogag
William H. Gogag
Han-Beng Gunn

S. Janis Hamilton
Cecilia Theresa Harry
Hazelton NITEP students
Heiltsuk Tribal Council
Dr and Mrs John Forbes Helliwell, OC
Hosem Enterprise
Investors Group Incorporated
Jackman Foundation
William Jeffrey
Mary Jane Joe
Francine N. Johnny
M. Audrey Johnson
Francis Johnson
Albert N. Johnston
Joseph S. Stauffer Foundation
Felicity Jules
Beverly A. Kakakaway
Kamloops Indian Band
Wilma Keitlah
Dr David M. Kennedy
Dr Verna J. Kirkness, CM
Kispiox Band Council
Iola Knight
Knox United Church
Björn Lauridsen
Lillooet Indian Band
Carol A. McCauley
Madeleine MacIvor
Sharon Mack
Hugh D. McLean
Dr John A. McLean
James Wilson McLeod
Janet McQueen
Lorna Jeanette Mathias

Donors, continued

The Architectural Team

First Nations House of Learning Objectives

Nathan Matthew
Jack Meier
Dr Helmut Meisl
Pamela June Miles
Helen Milosevich
Alice E. Moore
Barbara Morin
D. Shirley Morven
Ronald J. Neden
John and Catherine J. Newlands
Leonard Nicholson
Dr Robert Peter Nissen
James H. Norie
Francine Norris
North Thompson Indian Band
Oak Avenue United Church
Order of OMI in British
   Columbia
Valerie Overgaard
P. Lawson Travel
Dr K. George Pedersen, OC
Dr Penny Pedersen
Rolf N. Pedersen
Nancy Pennier
John Pichugin
Gwendolyn Rose Point
Marta M. Powell
Edmond E. Price
Manly Price
Province of British Columbia
Sylvia Linda Rickard
Wendy Robinson
Rev. Peter Rolston
Roman Catholic Archbishop of
   Vancouver

Roman Catholic Episcopal
   Corp, Prince Rupert
Marjorie Sandercock
Alfred and Joan Scow
Sechelt Indian Band
Colleen A. Seymour
Sharon United Church
Catherine Shultis
Sharon I. Shuter
Charles Skelton
Skidegate Band Council
Skowkale Administration
Gayle Patricia Smith
South Burnaby United Church
   Women
Justice J.E. Spencer
Squamish Indian Band
Dr Shirley Anne Sterling
Dawn L. Stevens
Mark L. Stevenson
Dr David Suzuki, OC, OBC
Dr Harry S. Swain
Gerrit and Sheila TeHennepe
Sarah TeHennepe
Donald Patrick J. Thomas
Dr Andrew Royden Thompson
Christine H. Thomson
Linda M. Tocher
John Wm Toovey
Catherine Trehearne
Elsie M. Turcotte
Vancouver School of Theology
James B. and Ilse Wallace
Dolly Beatrice Watts
Dr Deirdre M.S. Webster

West Point Grey United Church
Jennifer White
Margaret White
Pamela Wilson
Veronica Ann Wilson
Bruce Woodsworth
Jean T. York

Principal Architects:
Larry McFarland Architects Ltd
Larry McFarland
   (principal-in-charge)
David Wilkinson
   (project architect)
Peter Turje
Doug Walter
Richard Belli
Alfie Waugh
Don Lattman

Landscape Architect:
Christopher Phillips and
Associates

Structural Engineers:
Choukalos Woodburn
McKenzie & Miranda Ltd

Mechanical/Electrical
Engineers:
D.W. Thomson Consultants
Ltd

Builder:
Heatherbrae Construction
Co. Ltd

- to facilitate the participation
  of First Nations peoples in a
  wide range of study areas by
  providing information on postsecondary opportunities and
  by providing support services
  for students on campus
- to expand the range and depth
  of program and course offerings
  at UBC related to needs identified by First Nations people
  and communities in BC
- to identify, support, and promote research that would benefit First Nations
- to increase First Nations leadership on campus
- to maintain and expand the
  First Nations Longhouse to
  enhance access and support
  services for First Nations
  students
- to educate the university
  community and the wider
  community about First Nations
  issues and concerns
- to found an international
  component for the advancement
  of indigenous peoples around
  the world.